THE DRAMA OF ANCIENT ISRAEL

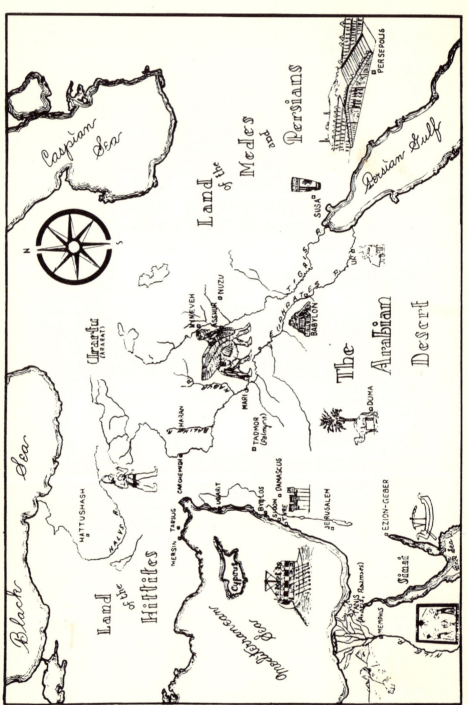

THE WORLD THAT SURROUNDED THE HEBREWS

The Drama of Ancient Israel

by

JOHN W. FLIGHT

SOPHIA L. FAHS
Collaborator

THE BEACON PRESS   •   BOSTON

Preface

IN A STUDY WHICH COVERS so long a period of time and touches so many difficult problems of historical, literary, and religious importance, it is quite impossible to express the indebtedness which this work owes to countless scholars who have labored in this field. A few footnotes indicate specific obligations to some of the more recent researches of Biblical scholars.

Sincere thanks are due especially to Mrs. Sophia Lyon Fahs, who has given unstintedly of her wisdom and experience to achieve an appropriate form of presentation for this story of Israel's national beginnings.

Since the book is one in the Beacon Series in Religious Education, it has profited in its preparation by the continued interest of the Rev. Ernest W. Kuebler, director of the Division of Education of the American Unitarian Association, and of the members of the Committee on Curriculum and Worship. We are indebted to them all for their readings of the manuscript and for their helpful criticisms.

Since the book is intended primarily for use by young people of junior and senior high-school age, it was most fortunate that, before the manuscript was sent to the printer, two teachers in the church school of Faith Church (Congregational), Springfield, Massachusetts were willing and able to use the manuscript experimentally with their classes. We are further gratified because Miss Elsie M. Bush, director of religious education in that church, on the basis of this experimental experience and in co-operation with us, has written the Teachers' Guide which accompanies this volume.

The imaginary interview with John Garstang at the beginning of Chapter 2 is used with the kind permission of Dr. Garstang.

Although the book has been written especially for young people, we believe it will prove to be of equal interest to adult Bible classes, to parents' groups, and to individual adults, especially to those who are eager to understand "the new Bible" that Biblical criticism and modern archaeological exploration have opened up for our generation. We have endeavored to use these findings of scientific men constructively, so that our readers may be led into a sympathetic understanding of the people of the Old Testament, their times, their religious outlook, and their beliefs, during the period covered by this book.

JOHN W. FLIGHT

Haverford

Pennsylvania

Contents

Illustrations

Why Retell This Ancient Drama?

THIS IS THE STORY of the making of the nation of Israel. The scene of the story is the country which is now known as Palestine, but which, about three thousand years ago, when the events described in this book took place, was called Canaan.

Throughout the centuries of known history, this small country has been a coveted land, not merely because it was once fertile, but because it is situated at the crossroads between Asia and Europe. Today Palestine has taken on unusual importance and is often in the news because some of the descendants of those people who first established the nation of Israel have gathered and organized a new Israel in that same land.

Thirty centuries ago and more, when the Hebrews began migrating into Canaan they found the country largely occupied by a people who were known as Canaanites and who were originally a Semitic people, as were the Hebrews. It has recently come as a surprise to Biblical scholars to discover that these Canaanites were really the people later named in our history books as the Phoenicians. We now know what our grandparents had no way of knowing — that, for several centuries before the Hebrews invaded the land, those ancient Phoenicians occupied a large and prosperous territory, much larger than is now included in Palestine. Theirs was not a kingdom with a single ruler but consisted of many city states, each with its own king. They were the people who first invented alphabetic writing. They were the people who later developed the art of sailing the seas in ships and of trading with the peoples of the world. In their achievement of a high degree of artistic skill and architecture, they rivaled their illustrious neighbors, the Egyptians.

At the time this story opens, however, during the reign of Pharaoh Akhenaten (beginning B.C.E. 1377), these Canaanites had already been weakened by several centuries of wars with the Pharaohs. Canaan had long been a part of the Egyptian Empire, and the Canaanites had become a subject people, divided and controlled by their conquerors, and required to pay heavy tribute to the Pharaohs.

At this time of weakness, a number of different Semitic tribes from the deserts to the north, east, and south of Canaan tried to invade the country. Some of these gave up the effort or became mixed with the Canaanites, while others appear to have joined forces with the Hebrews who migrated from Egypt under Moses. These succeeded in maintaining an identity separate from the Canaanites, though greatly influenced by the civilization and even by the religion of Canaan.

The most serious rival invaders to the Hebrews were the Philistines, who had been driven from their island home in the Mediterranean — probably Crete — and who had settled on the western shores of Palestine. These Philistines were a clever and strong people who had learned some of the arts and crafts of the Minoans on Crete. Indeed, the importance of the Philistines in the history of Canaan is shown by the fact that the name Palestine now given to the country means "the land of the Philistines."

The story of this book is a drama that spreads over five centuries. The final chapter presents the first great national tragedy. This tragedy was the first in a series of many tragedies that have plagued the progress of Israel from then until now. One of the bitterest of these tragedies was the downfall of Jerusalem to the Babylonians (586 B.C.E.). After that event, descendants of the Hebrews, known thereafter as Jews, became scattered in many countries around the Mediterranean. In succeeding centuries they continued to spread among all the nations of the globe. But through all these centuries some of them have kept alive the memory of the land of their fathers and have longed to return there to re-establish themselves once more as a nation. They did succeed in making a partial return when Cyrus of Persia conquered Babylon (B.C.E. 536) and still more Jews came back in the latter part of the fifth century B.C.E. Later they even achieved an independent Jewish kingdom for about a century, only to be conquered in turn by the Romans in 63 B.C.E. From that time on, there has been no independent Jewish nation until recently.

Why has this determined purpose to return to what they continue to call their "home land" never died? A person who wishes to understand the passionate fervor and persistence of this national hope needs to know, first of all, the ancient story in this book. It is not all that one should know in order to comprehend the intense emotions aroused by the struggle of the Jews to re-establish the Israeli nation. It is, however, an important part of the historical background, for it is the story of how that nation first came to be.

The main literary sources for the story told here are the books of Joshua, Judges, Samuel and Kings, as found in the Hebrew and Christian Bible. But it should be pointed out that the story as we tell it in this book is different in a number of important ways from the story as told in the Bible. The reason for this is that we have tried to recover as far as possible, what really happened in those far-off days. So much new knowledge about the Bible and its making has come to us in recent years that we cannot conscientiously accept as historically true all of the Bible record concerning this period as previous generations of Bible readers have done. In many cases there are two or more accounts of the same event, and these often disagree with one another. Most of the accounts were written long after the actual happenings by writers who interpreted and even changed or added to, the original story, according to their own later points of view. They did this in order to propagate certain beliefs, to exalt the past achievements of their own people, and to cast scorn upon their enemies, especially the Canaanites. As the Hebrew story-tellers retold the stories from generation to generation, they belittled all that pertained to those ancient foes, idealized their own early leaders, and exaggerated their achievements. But fortunately they let the older accounts stand side by side with their own later additions, so that we are able to recover most of the original story.

Archaeologists also have thrown much new light on the conditions in Canaan at that early time. They have unearthed in Palestine and Syria massive city walls, palaces, and temples which the Canaanites and Philistines built. They have found pottery, and beautifully carved ivory plaques, and clay tablets with writing on them. Many of these tablets were inscribed with prayers composed by Canaanite priests. It is these archaeologists who have brought forth evidence to show that the Canaanites and Philistines had developed many of the skills of civilized life before the

Israelite nation came into being. And judging from the Canaanite prayers that have been found, it is clear that at least some of the Canaanites' religious ideas and customs were adopted by the Hebrews. In fact, it is now known that the very form and style of Hebrew poetry in the Bible owes much to the Canaanite literary art of pre-Hebrew times.

In addition to the reconstruction of the story as given in this book, the story of the conquest of Canaan, as it is told in the Bible and as it has been commonly believed by generations of both Christians and Jews, needs to be understood. According to the old story, the Hebrews were commanded by their God to go into the land and take it away from the Canaanites. Since the Canaanites worshiped other gods, they were wicked people and should be completely destroyed. The Hebrews were regarded as God's "chosen people" and Canaan as the "promised land" — that is, God promised Canaan to Abraham and to all his descendants forever. As long as the Hebrews followed the directions their God gave for the conquest, they were successful. Whenever they failed, it was not because of the superior forces of the Canaanites but because the Hebrews had been disobedient to their God. The point of view represented by this Bible story assumed that God could and would perform miracles for the special benefit of those whom he had chosen, as long as they followed his directions.

Our book has been written in order to set forth what appears actually to have happened. We distinguish this from what was believed in those early days of three thousand years ago. We believe it is important that the historical facts should be sifted from the mass of legends that have accumulated around them. We fully recognize that the religious point of view and beliefs of those ancient heroes of Israel, and even of the later storytellers, represent early stages in the religion of the Bible. We have not assumed that this or any other aggressive warfare is right or wrong, or that the beliefs or deeds of those early heroes are all worthy to be imitated today.

This dramatic saga is presented as a series of essentially true experiences in human history. We think it is important that Christians and Jews of our day be intelligent about these experiences, because Judaism and Christianity and the whole of Western civilization have been greatly influenced by the emotional inheritance from these events.

In reading the story, we should keep in mind the ambitions of the Canaanites and the Philistines as well as those of the Hebrews. We should realize that many of the beliefs and practices of all these ancient peoples were limited in their range and quality by the times in which they lived. Such beliefs fitted the general unscientific and narrow historical outlook upon life and the universe which these people then had. One should consider the pros and cons of the whole situation. Why did these people do as they did? Do similar problems face us today? In the light of the larger range of knowledge and understanding available to us, how are we going to solve our problems? This *Drama of Ancient Israel* is a story which both Christians and Jews may well ponder.

THE DRAMA OF ANCIENT ISRAEL

1

A Great People in Danger

ON A DAY LONG AGO, in the fourteenth century B.C.E., this ancient drama began. Ebed-Hepa, governor of the walled city of Uru-salim,[1] was pacing restlessly back and forth in his audience room. He was about to dictate a letter to his scribe, who sat cross-legged on the floor before him. With a soft clay tablet on one knee and a reed stylus in his hand, the scribe was waiting to write down the message his master was about to send.

Ebed-Hepa had been talking with his trusted scribe about the danger that threatened their city. "This letter must go at once to Pharaoh Akhenaten of Egypt. Only he who is now the great Lord and Ruler of all Canaan can help us. Unless the Pharaoh sends us help soon, our city will be captured by these barbarous bands from the desert who are raiding our lands."

"Yes, my lord," the scribe said quietly, "if your humble servant may speak — only a few days ago we heard that these barbarians had plundered Rubudu and the lands around it. That means that they are coming nearer to us. But perhaps our city is strong enough to resist them."

The governor shook his head and went on: "No, I fear the worst, for we have not soldiers enough to defend ourselves. And these desert men will stop at nothing. We simply must have help. The Pharaoh promised soldiers to protect us. He owes us this, for we have never failed to pay our taxes. But where are the soldiers? In my grandfather's day the Egyptians kept strong armies in all our cities. But now, just when we need protection most, we have no help from Egypt."

As the governor paused, his scribe ventured to speak again: "My lord, what's wrong with this new Pharaoh, Akhenaten? Doesn't he care any longer about this land his grandfather con-

[1] Called Jerusalem in later times.

3

quered? Is he going to leave us all to the mercy of these wild invaders?"

"That I cannot tell," replied Ebed-Hepa, "but it begins to look so. Other governors have written him for help, but it has never come. The city of Rubudu, which you say has fallen to these destroyers, need never have been lost had there been even a small well-armed force of Egyptian guardsmen to defend it."

There was silence for some moments. The scribe seemed about to speak again, when the governor said: "If we can make the Pharaoh see clearly how seriously we are threatened, perhaps he will send archers to defend our walls. He must not let this, his largest city in this district, be lost. I will speak plainly to him. Write this for me, my good scribe, and address it to the Pharaoh's own secretary:

> Speak to the king, my lord. Thus says Ebed-Hepa, thy servant; at the feet of my lord, the king, seven and seven times I prostrate myself. Thou dost not harken to me! Let the king send soldiers to me. There will be no lands left to the king, my lord. The Habiru [2] are plundering all the lands of the king, my lord. If soldiers are sent this year, then there will be lands left to the king, my lord. But if no soldiers come, the lands of the king will be lost. . . .
>
> Verily, the king has set his name upon Urusalim forever. Therefore, he cannot abandon the lands of Urusalim. . . .
>
> Unto the scribe of the king, my lord, I write. I am Ebed-Hepa, thy servant. Take these plain words to the king, my lord. All the lands of the king, my lord, are going to ruin.

One sunshiny morning some weeks later, Akhenaten, the great Pharaoh of Upper and Lower Egypt, was sitting in the council room of his palace in the city of Thebes. His patient scribe was waiting to read the royal mail. The letters were not written with ink on white parchment. The words in these letters had been scratched into soft clay tablets that had afterwards hardened. The tablets were piled like baked mud pies on a small table before the scribe.

"My lord, the king, all these tablets on the table here this

---

[2] Most scholars think that *Habiru* was a general term used to describe all the desert nomads who were sweeping into Canaan. The people we know as Hebrew were one group among these many related tribes.

PHARAOH AKHENATEN
A sculptured head made about 1360 B.C.E.

morning have come from the land of Canaan. Each tablet is marked by the name of a king of some city in that country."

"You have read all those letters to me before," said the Pharaoh Akhenaten impatiently. "Why should I hear them again? I have told you over and over that I am not interested in sending any soldiers to that far-away country."

"But, your Majesty," begged the scribe, "these are more recent letters, which I have not read you before. They are frightening letters, my lord. The Egyptian Empire is in danger. You must not forget that the Pharaohs before you conquered the land of Canaan. For many years now you have been receiving tribute from these foreign kings, and they were promised the protection of the Egyptian armies in return. The honor of my lord, the king, is at stake."[3]

"Read the letters then if you must," said the Pharaoh. "But I tell you now I am not interested in doing what they ask."

The scribe, glad to have his master's permission to read the letters, picked up one of the clay tablets. "This is from Ebed-Hepa, king of Urusalim. Listen well, my lord! 'The Habiru are plundering all the lands of the king, my lord. If no soldiers are come, all the lands of the king, my lord, will be lost.' Those are strong words my lord," said the scribe. "They are the words of a man who is desperate."

Pharaoh Akhenaten thumped his fingers nervously on the arm of his chair. Why should he hold on to those lands far away that his great-great-grandfather had once conquered? Upper and Lower Egypt were large enough for Akhenaten. He did not believe in fighting in order to have a great empire anyway. He was building a new city that needed no armies to protect it! And the great temple of his dreams was not yet finished. Akhenaten had no time for foreign conquests. The priests of the old temples in Thebes were giving him all the trouble he could face.

Besides all this, the people of Canaan were a civilized people.

---

[3] From about 1550 to about 1225 B.C.E., Canaan remained an Egyptian province except for brief rebellions. Thutmose III during his reign (1490-1436) campaigned over and over again in Canaan to put down these rebellions, and was successful. When Akhenaten ascended the throne in 1377, however, the Egyptian forces in Canaan were greatly weakened, because he was not interested in wars and empire or in enlarging the Egyptian Empire. This, therefore, was a favorable time for an invasion.

A LETTER FROM EBED-HEPA

The king of Jerusalem is asking Pharaoh Akhenaten for help against the Habiru.
This clay tablet was found at Tel-el-Amarna (the modern name for the City-of-
the-Horizon in Egypt).

They were not barbarians. Akhenaten knew that well. Why could they not protect themselves? Urusalim was a walled city, and there were twenty other such walled cities in their land. Let their kings get together and do their own fighting.

The Canaanites were good archers, too. Had they forgotten their skills with bow and arrow? Surely the Egyptians had not taken this from the Canaanites. Oh, why had the Pharaohs before him ever conquered that far-away land?

Akhenaten brusquely dismissed his scribe. "I told you when you began that I was not interested."

The faithful scribe picked up his pile of clay letters and walked out of the room.

The letter from Ebed-Hepa was never answered. Nor were the other letters from the other kings of Canaan's cities.

Rumors Spread among the Habiru

Rumors were passed along from one desert tribe to another east of the Jordan River. Travelers said, "The cities of Canaan are not so strongly defended as they once were. Their Egyptian conquerors have deserted them. Once they supplied soldiers for the Canaanites. They sent archers to guard the city walls. But now the Canaanites no longer have armies to protect them."

Such rumors were good news to the wandering shepherds who for years had been trying to eke out a sparse living from the desert lands east and south of Canaan. They had often listened with envy to travelers' tales of the great walled cities. Living in a house with walls and roof, not far off from other people and with a high stone wall around all the houses together! How safe a person would feel! And how comfortable and easy life would be! No wild animals to frighten you! No moving about! No pulling up of tents and hiking off, no one knew where, to begin all over again!

And what wonderful things these traveling men brought back with them from this country of cities and cultivated fields and gardens! Big bags full of barley and oats! Large baskets of grapes and olives! Why shouldn't more of the desert men cross the Jordan River and plunder those fields of grain and those vineyards and olive orchards?

So one party of wild shepherds after another dared to cross

the Jordan. They would steal into the fields and vineyards at night, gather as much grain and fruit as they could carry off, and then they would hide or hurry back across the river where they were again safe. Some settled down to live in the hills outside the towns.

As the years passed, many raiding parties of shepherds crossed over into Canaan. Some raided one town and some another. Some came from the deserts in the south. Others came from the dry lands east of the Jordan River.

Barbarous Habiru! Hebrew wild men! Call them by either name. To the Canaanites they were all the same. Barbarians of whom the city people were afraid.

Yet for some reason the different kings of these different walled cities in Canaan seemed unable to get together and plan an effective fight. They had depended so long on the Egyptians to decide things for them that now there was no person among them ready to take the lead. No one felt duty-bound to call the kings together and make them work out a plan and fight together against the invaders. So the rough, plain men of the deserts had their chance.

During the hundred years between 1400 B.C.E. and 1300 B.C.E., this was the state of affairs in the land of Canaan. It is not difficult to understand why Ebed-Hepa was so greatly alarmed as he saw one after another of the Habiru tribes make their way into the land.[4]

---

[4] The story in this chapter is based on certain clay letters found by the archaeologists in the ruins of Pharaoh Akhenaten's new City-of-the-Horizon. The place is now called Tell-el-Amarna.

2

The Walls of Jericho

In the Year 1932

It was a busy-looking place out there on the sandy hillside west of the modern city of Jericho. A few plain temporary houses squatted on the barren sand. Beside them was a big mound or cluster of mounds that had been partly dug out. Men with loaded baskets were coming up out of the big holes while others were going down into the holes.

An auto loaded with tourists passed by on the road. Curious to learn what this digging was all about, they got out of their car and walked over to the mound to look around.

Spying a man who appeared to be in charge, the leader of the group walked up to him and began questioning him. "Good morning, sir. What are you doing here?"

"We're digging into this mound to find out what really happened to the walls of ancient Jericho," said the man. "I'm an archaeologist from England. My name is John Garstang. This is now the fourth winter we have been digging into this mound."

The tourist was puzzled. "You mean to say that you have been working here for four years digging into this pile of dirt just to find out whether or not that old Bible story about the walls of Jericho tumbling down is really true?"

"Exactly so," said Dr. Garstang. "But it's more than that, sir. These things that we find down under these layers and layers of rubbish and sand, that have been piling up for centuries — these things have history written on them. These pieces of pottery — such as that man there is carrying out of the hole — people once used. Opening this mound is like opening a book of history. And the book always speaks the truth."

"But it must take a lot of patience to learn to read such a big book, doesn't it, Doctor? And plain, hard, dirty work, too?"

10

Dr. Garstang smiled. "Yes, of course," he said. "But it's very exciting now and then. When you find the walls of an old city or the walls of an old house, you feel as though you were stepping right into the old city or house. And when you find big jars that were once full of wheat or barley, or you find burnt-up onions or dates or even some hard bread dough laid out ready to put into the oven, then the people of long ago who used these things seem almost alive again. They become real people."

"Have you found anything exciting yet, Doctor?" asked the tourist.

"Would you like to see some of our finds? My wife will be glad to show them to you if you will go over there to that house down the hill. She and I and the helpers we have trained have handled and cleaned and marked about a hundred thousand pieces of pottery in the last four years. Some of these we have been able to piece together into the vases and jars and bowls and pots they once were."

The visitors looked surprised. One hundred thousand pieces! Had they heard correctly?

"Before you go, however," said Dr. Garstang, "let me show you around the mound a little. It's the walls, you remember, that were so important in the old story."

"Yes, I recall the story," said the tourist, as the company walked over to the eastern side of the mound. "The Hebrew army marched round the city seven times, and when the priests blew their trumpets, the walls just fell down flat. It was a big miracle."

"Well," said Dr. Garstang, "something happened that was very extraordinary."

"Really?" said the tourist. "You don't mean to say you have proved that the miracle really happened, do you, Doctor?"

"Oh, no!" said Dr. Garstang. "Archaeologists don't talk or think in terms of miracles. We are simply trying to find out what really happened. See the ruins of those walls there! See what is left of that other wall some twenty feet away from the first wall? Notice how the stones lie about in disorder. And how in this other place you find a piece of wall standing quite straight. Those are big stones at the bottom! Little stones here and there between the big ones and even bricks on top! In some places we found stone steps on the inside of the walls leading to the top, and we found signs that houses had been built on top of the walls!"

"How old do you figure the city was when these walls were standing?"

"We can't say definitely just when the walls were built. They are very, very old. But we do feel quite sure about the time when these walls tumbled down."

"When was that, Dr. Garstang?"

"We think it was some time before or perhaps during the reign of Akhenaten of Egypt in the fourteenth century B.C.E."

"How very interesting!" said the tourist. "We have just been in Egypt and visited the museum where those beautiful pieces of art from Akhenaten's City-of-the-Horizon are displayed. But, Doctor, how in the world can you figure out these dates? Of course, I know that the farther down you dig the older things must be. But how old? How do you tell?"

"Well, we were fortunate this time. We found a cemetery just outside the city — down in that valley," he said, pointing to the north. "We found many interesting things there — necklaces of bone and carnelian and swords of bronze, and fifteen hundred pieces of unbroken pottery. But, what was most important, we found scarabs. Each scarab had the name of a Pharaoh on it. We figured out how old the pottery alongside those scarabs was, and then we compared that pottery and its designs with broken pottery with the same designs found inside the city."

"What patience an archaeologist must have!" exclaimed the tourist. "Aren't you bored sometimes?"

"Yes, it's tedious. It's like working out a gigantic jigsaw puzzle. But now and then it's very exciting!"

"And what do you think made the walls of Jericho fall down, Doctor?" asked the tourist.

"I'm convinced it was a big earthquake. A similar earthquake occurred in this region not many years ago.

"Then the earthquake must have been followed by a great fire. The whole city seems to have been burnt. We have found ashes and burnt beams everywhere. And it all must have happened so quickly that the people in the city had to flee without being able to carry off their food. Nor have we found any signs of the city having been looted."

"This is very exciting," said the tourist. "But what do you

AN ARAB CAMP
The camp of the Habiru beside the Jordan River must have looked much like this Arab camp of today.

think the Hebrews had to do with destroying the city, Doctor?"

"Why not go to your hotel," said Dr. Garstang, "and get out your Bibles and read the first few chapters in Joshua and figure out for yourselves what might have happened. This is an example of what archaeologists can do for you. They can help you to sift out the facts of history and separate them from the legends that were told to explain the facts. But first you should go to the house and see our exhibition."

So the party bade the patient doctor good-by and walked down the hill to see for themselves what the archaeologists had found in the ancient mound.

During the Fourteenth Century B.C.E.[1]

Several thousand Hebrews were encamped on the eastern shore of the Jordan River just north of the Dead Sea. They were commanded by a certain daring chieftain whose name we do not know.[2] These wandering herdsmen were determined to get into that fertile land of cities and gardens called Canaan. They had had enough of wandering in the hot, dry wastelands of the desert. They even had the boldness to think they could capture one of the big walled cities of Canaan if they schemed wisely. Their chieftain had inspired them with a great courage.

Now, before the spring rains, the Jordan River can usually be easily forded at this place just above the Dead Sea where the Hebrew shepherds were camping. But when these Hebrews actually reached the shores of the Jordan, they were surprised to find that the river was already in flood, and the waters were deep.

Day after day, they waited anxiously. But day after day the river continued to run deep, making an impassable barrier before them. Often in the evenings their chieftain would sit in council with other leaders around him, and they would talk.

"We cannot wait here indefinitely," he said one evening. "This flooded river means that the early rains have begun in the north,

---

[1] The following episode is entirely imaginary. It is used with Dr. Garstang's kind permission. It is based upon his findings in Jericho and on our own study of the Bible record. This is found in the Book of Joshua, chapters 2, 3, 4, and 6.

[2] In the Bible record the name of the chieftain is given as Joshua, the successor of Moses. According to our reckoning of dates, the tribes from Egypt came into Canaan about one hundred years later.

and more water will be coming down each day until the rains stop."

The discouraged men in the circle were shaking their heads. One cried out, "If only we could have reached here a few days earlier, before the rains started!"

The chief went on. "There's no use complaining, my brothers. Let us wait here another day or two. Then if our scouts cannot find a way for us to cross the river, we shall have to go northward or eastward. We can not go back to the desert from which we have come. There will surely be some grazing places still open to us on this side of the river."

"What our chief has said is the best we can do now," said another. "But we must not give up our aim to get across the river just as soon as we can after the floods have gone down. You know, my brothers, that we have been hoping for this opportunity for a long time. And just now there are no Egyptian garrisons to keep us out. The people in the walled cities are too weak to defend themselves or their surrounding lands."

Once more the chief spoke. "There is one strongly walled city, which the Canaanites call Jericho, that lies just beyond this river. We must take this city if there is any way to do it, for it guards all the roads leading into other parts of the land. It would be foolish to leave such a strong city in enemy hands if we wish to settle anywhere beyond."

A look of uneasiness passed over the faces of the others when they heard this. They waited for their chief to suggest what he thought could be done. He went on: "We must send spies across the river to go into the city and see what the defenses are. They may be able to discover a weak spot in the walls, or to find someone inside the city who will help us to enter by surprise. The spies can swim across the river even while the waters are high. If the river goes down in a day or two, we shall be prepared to follow them, and to try capturing the city."

Spies Enter Jericho

It was hard to imagine that these poorly armed desert men would ever be able to take such a strongly defended city, but the chief's plan seemed a wise one. So the next morning two spies swam across the swollen river, and walked the few miles to the city of Jericho. They stole into the city before the gates were closed, and found shelter in the home of a woman named Rahab, whose house was built on top of the broad city wall.

"I have heard about your people," said Rahab to the spies, "and I know how strong you are. All the people of this city, even our leaders, are afraid of you. They fear that you will do what other men from the desert have been doing to other cities on this side of the Jordan." She paused, and looked troubled and thoughtful. "These people of Jericho have not been friendly toward me and my family, but if you will deal kindly with me, I will help you to take the city. . . ."

She had hardly finished speaking when there came a knock on her door and voices shouting: "Open the door! We must search your house!"

"They are the king's guards!" she whispered excitedly to the Hebrew spies. "Someone has told them that you have come to my house! Be quick! Follow me." And she led them up to the flat roof and hid them under a pile of drying flax-stalks.

She then went back downstairs to greet the city guards at the door. "Bring out the two men who are in your house!" they demanded. "We must have them. They are spies."

Rahab answered: "Yes, two men did come to my house, but I did not know who they were or where they came from. They have gone now. Just before the city gates were closed for the night, they went away. If you will follow them quickly, you may overtake them."

The guards left at once in pursuit. As soon as they had gone, Rahab returned to the roof to speak with the spies.

"If you will promise me," she said to them, "that when you have taken the city you will deal kindly with me and my family, as I have done to you, I will help you capture this city."

They promised that they would do so, and Rahab brought a rope by which the men might let themselves down out of a window of her house to the ground outside the city wall. She cautioned them: "Go into the hills to the west of the city so that the guards will not find you. They will be pursuing you eastward in the direction of the Jordan. Hide there for three days before going back to your people."

As the two spies departed, one of them produced a red cord

JERICHO

A drawing of the city as it may have been in Joshua's time, by Mabel Ratcliffe, a member of John Garstang's expedition. From The Story of Jericho. Used by permission.

which he had concealed in his robe. He said to Rahab: "When we come back here with our people to attack the city, take this scarlet cord and hang it outside your window. Then our men will know which house is yours and will spare it and your family."

Meanwhile the Hebrews encamped on the other side of the Jordan River waited impatiently. Two days passed, then three. They wondered what had happened to their two brothers. How excited they were when on the fourth day the two spies returned and reported what they had done!

"It should be easy for us to capture the city," they said as they finished telling of their adventure, "for now we have someone to help us get inside the city walls by surprise, if the river goes down to permit our crossing. Rahab has told us exactly where the weakest part of the wall is, and just what we must do to enter it."

The Great Surprise

On hearing this encouraging report, the whole camp became restless, eager to cross over at once. But the river was still in flood. Then came the great surprise. The Hebrews did not know it, but at about the time the spies returned to camp, a remarkable thing was happening upstream in the Jordan — something that has occurred only two or three times since, as far as we know. About fifteen miles north, it seems, a landslide, caused either by heavy rains or by an earthquake, threw many tons of rocks from a high cliff right down into a narrow part of the river. These rocks formed a dam across the river to the cliffs on either side, and stopped the flow of the water.

The next morning, on going down to the river, the Hebrews could hardly believe their eyes. For they saw a river entirely emptied of water, and the rocks and mud on the bottom uncovered. Their chief lost no time in ordering the entire camp to break up. With women and children, tents and supplies, they all walked down into the stony river bed and crossed over safely to the other side.

About five miles beyond them lay the city of Jericho and a few men were sent ahead to see what was going on there. In a surprisingly short time the men returned, so filled with excitement that they could hardly speak. Breathlessly one of them shouted: "The wall — it is down — the eastern wall — all is confusion inside the city!" The same earthquake that had caused the landslide upstream had also shaken down part of the city wall. Now was their opportunity. "We must take advantage of the panic inside the city," the chief commanded. "Let all our fighting men storm the city and take possession!"

It seemed too wonderful to be true that poorly armed men from the desert should thus be able to enter and capture such a strong fortress as Jericho.

The story as it is in the Bible says that nothing was spared in Jericho, and that the Hebrew attackers "utterly destroyed all that was in the city, both man and woman, young and old, and ox and sheep and ass, with the edge of the sword." But "the young men, the spies, went in and brought out Rahab and her father, and mother, and kinsmen and all that she had. . . . They put them in a place of security outside the camp of Israel. And they burnt the city with fire, and all that was in it." ³ It was "total war" as we have come to know it in the Second World War — so complete and ruthless that nothing remained but rubble and ruin. And the city of Jericho was not rebuilt and occupied again for five hundred years.⁴

---

3 Joshua 6: 21, 23, 24.
4 I Kings 16:34.

3

Friends or Enemies—Which?

JUST WHAT OTHER BIG CITIES these early conquerors of Jericho may have taken in the new land, we do not know. They were but one group of tribes among many that were sweeping into the land of Canaan during the fourteenth century B.C.E. Some came from the south. Some came from the north and some from across the Jordan River. We might say that all these invaders were related to one another, since they all belonged to a large group of Semitic-speaking people inhabiting the Near East. For many years they had led their separate tribal lives, many of them as wanderers in the desert spaces. They had even fought each other, for it was often a matter of life or death to determine which tribes could keep possession of the few fertile spots in the desert.

It was not until over a hundred years later that the Hebrew group which had lived as slaves in Egypt tried also to invade Canaan.[1] Under the strong leadership of Moses, they had escaped into the desert of Arabia. There they had wandered from oasis to oasis for many years. Moses himself had died; but a strong leader named Joshua had taken his place. The city of Jericho had probably lain in ruins for over a hundred years before this group of tribes under Joshua came marching into Canaan. To the Canaanites already living in the land, these different desert tribes were all alike. They were the "barbarous Habiru," whose rugged strength and determination the Canaanites feared.

The Hebrew group under Joshua, although small in numbers, became the most important of all these Semitic invaders in the ancient drama of this book, because it was this group that finally became the leader of all the other invaders. Since the men who wrote the story of the invasion of Canaan, as it is in the Bible, belonged to this particular group, it was quite natural

[1] We are following in general the dating advocated by Dr. W. F. Albright, noted archaeologist, and suggested earlier, with some differences, by Dr. T. J. Meek in Chapter 1 of his *Hebrew Origins*.

that they should give credit for the biggest exploits to Joshua and his men. According to certain parts of the Bible story, the tribes under Joshua destroyed all the important cities of Canaan and divided up the land among the twelve tribes by casting lots for the different sections.[2] This story of the quick and complete conquest under a single leader is now known to be a great exaggeration.

The truth about the conquest seems to be that a few other cities near-by Jericho were probably taken by the Hebrews under Joshua, and these cities were completely destroyed — that is, they were burnt to ashes and rubble. One of these was probably Bethel, not far to the northwest of Jericho. (It is confused with Ai in Joshua 7-8.) Two important walled cities in the south, Lachish and Debir, were also destroyed at about this same time. Many scholars think that the Hebrews were probably the conquerors. Aside from these cities, however, we know of no others of importance that the Hebrews actually destroyed or took over during Joshua's lifetime. Even the Bible narrative itself in the Book of Judges tells of many cities and districts from which the Canaanites were not driven out, but where the Hebrews settled down and lived with these older inhabitants.[3]

Apparently for a long time each tribe fought its own way into the land and settled down wherever it was possible to gain a foothold. Now and then one tribe joined with others, but sometimes they even fought one another for a place to live. The situation was very much like that of the thirteen original colonies in America before 1776. They, too, were independent of one another, sometimes even jealous of one another. It took a long time for the colonies to come together to "form a more perfect union;" they had to learn through many hardships the lesson that "in unity there is strength." It was much the same with the Hebrew tribes in Canaan. Not at once did they gather their forces under one leader. In fact, two hundred years passed before they presented a united front against the Canaanites.

Evidently there were two theories about the way to conquer the land. One was to make friends with the older inhabitants

[2] Book of Joshua, Chapter 21: 43-45; also the preceding chapters from 14 through 21.
[3] Judges 1: 19, 21, 27-34; Joshua 15: 63; 16: 10; 17: 12-13.

and push their way in with as little fighting as possible. The other theory was to attack one city after the other and to drive out or kill all the older inhabitants, and to completely destroy everything that belonged to them. The first of these two ways was, of course, the simpler and, as things turned out, it usually proved to be the more successful.

Sometimes the Canaanites were frightened by stories they heard of the cruel destruction of such cities as Jericho, and made the way easier for the newcomers. This probably did not happen often and when it did the story was news.[4]

The Trickery of the Gibeonites

An example of this kind of easy conquest occurred when the people of a town called Gibeon, about thirty miles west of the Jordan River, decided to make terms with the newcomers under Joshua. These Gibeonites chose a curious way to accomplish their purpose. They sent some of their own older men to the camp of Joshua as ambassadors. They came dressed in worn, tattered clothing and leading donkeys loaded with leaky wine-skins and with patched sacks containing dry, moldy bread. Thus they pretended to come from a distant part of the country and not from the near-by town of Gibeon.

Appearing weary and travel-stained before Joshua, the men from Gibeon said: "We have come from a far country and carry a message of peace to you. . . . We have heard of your great power and how you left Egypt because your God was mightier than the Pharaoh and the gods of Egypt. . . . So our leaders and people told us to go out to meet you before you came to our country, and to say to us, 'We are your servants; make a league with us.' We took this bread hot from our ovens when we left home; see how dry and moldy it is now, because we have come so far; see how these wineskins, which were new when we started out, are all leaky and broken; and see how old and ragged our shoes and clothes are from our long journey."

Strange to say, Joshua was convinced that these men had traveled a very great distance. He decided that it would be very fine if, by making an agreement with these men, he could add over a thousand people to his fighting force without having to

---

[4] Joshua, chapter 9.

A CANAANITE FARMER
On this ivory plaque from Megiddo, a farmer proudly displays his ducks.

make any struggle. And how good it would be to have a friendly place in which to settle when he and his people would reach the country from which he supposed these Gibeonites had come. So he made a treaty with the men. He and the other chiefs with him took an oath in the name of Yahweh that they would not harm these weary travelers or their people.

Three days later, however, Joshua found out that a trick had been played on him, that the city of Gibeon was near-by. Rumor of this false treaty spread throughout the camp, and many of the Hebrews shouted angrily for the death of the Gibeonite ambassadors.

But Joshua said, "No! We have given them our word in the name of Yahweh and we will keep it."

In the end it proved to be a good thing for the Hebrews to have made this treaty, for they found that the Gibeonites occupied three or four important cities which were along the roads leading into the country beyond, both to the west and to the south.

But there were those who reproved Joshua for having made friends with the Gibeonites. They realized that it might prove dangerous. They insisted that if the land was ever to be theirs, they would have to drive out the Canaanites.

The God of the Desert and the Gods of the Land

This Hebrew group under Joshua, although small in number, became the most important of all these Semitic invaders in the ancient drama of this book. The reason for this may be found in the kind of religious beliefs which they had. Their great leader Moses had inspired them with a strong belief in a God who, they felt, was in a special way their own God. They called him Yahweh, which meant The-One-Who-Causes-To-Be-What-Comes-Into-Existence.[5] In other words, these Hebrews believed that Yahweh, their God, was the Creator of earth and sky and all that lives, and that he was therefore the greatest of all possible gods. These Hebrews had come to believe also that this great God had promised to help them conquer the land of Canaan provided they would worship him only and do as he commanded. This belief often made these invaders into fighters who might well be feared.

Some of these Hebrews, however, pushed their way into the country without fighting and lived peacefully in the Canaanite towns or settled down on some vacant plot of land nearby. Knowing little or nothing about farming, these Hebrews were quick to learn from watching and listening to the older inhabitants. But the Canaanites, on their part, taught the new arrivals many other things beside how to win a livelihood out of the soil. Sometimes these other things learned proved to be quite serious matters.

We can imagine two of these neighbors, a Hebrew and a Canaanite farmer, talking over their problems. "What is the best way to plant and care for my barley field," asks the Hebrew, "and why has my crop been so poor this year?" The Canaanite asks a few questions, and in return tells his Hebrew neighbor certain rules about planting. Then he comes to the most important advice of all. He says:

"Here in this land, whenever we plant seeds, we make a sacrifice at the village shrine to the God of the land. The God is the real owner of the land. That is why we call him the Baal. Our Baal is one of the sons of the great God El—God of all the earth and sky. Our Baal is strong. He can make the barley grow or not as he chooses. Perhaps if you will make friends with the Baal of this place your crops will be better. It may be, because you have not done this, that the Baal has become angry and has sent a pest to destroy your barley plants. Why don't you

---

[5] William F. Albright, *From the Stone Age to Christianity.* Baltimore: Johns Hopkins Press, 1940), p. 198.

try making a sacrifice on the altar under the great oak tree on the hill?"

The Hebrew farmer decides to do as the Canaanite farmer advises. Perhaps this particular year he succeeds in raising a very fine growth of barley. Now he is persuaded that the Baal has been at least partly responsible for what has happened. As a result he begins to wonder.

Could it be that Yahweh was merely the God of the desert where his people used to live? And that the gods that really counted in Canaan were those that the Canaanites had been worshiping for many centuries? Perhaps Yahweh could help the growing of flocks of sheep in the desert—yet what did he have to do with the growing of barley crops in Canaan? Perhaps Yahweh had gone back to Mount Sinai, where he had first made himself known to Moses. It must be that in Canaan the Baals were the gods who gave success to farmers.

Many of the Hebrews paid more attention to the Baals than to Yahweh, and they worshiped these gods in the many "high places" on the tops of hills where altars were to be found. To be sure, not all of the Hebrews did these things. Some of them kept their greatest loyalty for Yahweh alone, worshiping him only, and looking only to him for help in times of need. In some places they even used the hilltop altars of the Baals and made them into shrines for Yahweh. Some of them went so far as to call Yahweh the one great Baal.

New Laws Are Needed Too

Little by little, as one generation followed another, the Hebrews in Canaan came more and more to follow the customs of their neighbors. Some of them even married Canaanites, so that in time the two peoples, in parts of the country at least, could hardly be distinguished. So life in Canaan became different in many ways from what it had been in the desert.

As long as the Hebrews wandered over the deserts as shepherds, their pasture lands, their herds and flocks belonged to the whole tribe and not to any one family. As shepherds they set up camp near some stream or spring, let their animals graze on the hillsides around until the grass was eaten short; then the whole camp would pull up the stakes of their tents and move to a new oasis. The tribal chief decided all the important matters, and any one who dared to disobey the tribal rules was severely punished. Sometimes the offender was expelled from the tribe and made to wander off into the desert by himself. Sometimes he was even put to death.

But here in Canaan, life for the Hebrews was very different. Each tribe settled down wherever it was able to get possession. These different tribes were scattered over many miles of country. Some lived in villages and towns, others lived outside the towns in the country near-by, where they began the business of raising crops of barley and wheat. Some settlers prospered. Their crops grew large. Their herds of cattle and their flocks of sheep and goats increased. Others, less ambitious, were contented to work simply as hired laborers. In this way some of the Hebrews became rich landowners, while others remained poor, owning no land at all.

In this new situation, therefore, the Hebrews found it necessary to make new laws to meet these new conditions. For example, suppose an ox belonging to one man broke into another man's barley field or vineyard and ruined the growing crops—what should be done? Or suppose two oxen belonging to two different owners began fighting, the one ox gored the other ox? Or suppose a man's wife was hurt by his neighbor's ox? Or suppose two men quarreled over the boundaries between their separate fields? Or suppose a poor man needed to borrow something from a rich man—what could the rich man require the poor man to give? Naturally, in their new conditions, the Hebrews needed to work out new laws; and since the Canaanites had had long experience living on the land, and had already worked out rather good laws, the Hebrews copied many of the Canaanite laws.[6]

A New Temple in Shiloh

Others, however, were deeply disturbed by these changes and opposed them. Joshua had warned the people that they should be loyal to the God that Moses had taught them to pray to,

---

[6] Some of these new laws, though perhaps not quite in their present form, are recorded in Exodus, chapter 21; and 22: 1-17. See also Julius A. Bewer's *The Literature of the Old Testament* (revised edition; New York: Columbia University Press, 1947), pp. 30-42.

THE GOD BA-AL
The God hurls a thunderbolt and holds the lightning.
A stone stele engraved by a Canaanite.

or else they would be punished. In order to make this loyalty easier, a small temple was built to Yahweh in a town called Shiloh in the very center of this hill country. A man was appointed to live in the temple and to be the priest. Animals were slain on the stone altar and worshipers often gave part of the meat to Yahweh as a gift and a prayer.

It was here that they brought the sacred box or ark which they had carried with them ever since their departure from the sacred mountain, Sinai.[7] They still thought of Yahweh as having his home in the south, at the sacred mountain; but so long as they had the ark, they felt that Yahweh was with them, and that he would help them whenever they were in great need or danger.

In course of time, this new sacred place came to mean so much to the descendants of the tribes who had entered the land under Joshua, and to some of the other Hebrew tribes as well, that gradually there were men from other tribes who came to consult the one God, Yahweh, at Shiloh. This step was very important, for it encouraged the growth of the scattered, independent tribes toward nationhood, by giving them a common loyalty, a sort of brotherhood in religion, to bind them together. It may be that here, for the first time, the name "Israel" should be given to this growing federation of Hebrew tribes in Canaan.

But many years must pass, many more hard battles must be fought, many disappointments and even struggles between these brother tribes must take place, before these people from the desert became permanently at home in the new land.

---

[7] John W. Flight, *Moses: Egyptian Prince, Nomad Sheikh, Lawgiver* (Boston: Beacon Press, 1942), p. 117.

4

Battling for the Plain of Esdraelon

The Pleasant Valley

Years passed by. The old chief Joshua was dead. The tribe he had led into Canaan had settled down for the most part in small hamlets in the hill country of central Canaan. They now regarded these hills as so definitely their own that they had named this part of the country Ephraim, after the name of their ancestor Ephraim, one of the sons of Jacob.[1]

Other tribes, closely related to these Ephraimites, had settled further north on the hillsides around the Sea of Galilee. They, too, had staked out their claims to the land they occupied, each tribe naming its conquered spot after its own ancestor. Issachar, Zebulon, Naphtali, were the tribes around the lake to the north.

But between these two general groups of settlers, and separating them from each other, was a wide fertile plain, called the Plain of Esdraelon. This valley stretched across the country from the Mediterranean Sea to the Jordan River. Here in this pleasant land, thousands of Canaanites lived peacefully in a row of walled cities, two of which were especially famous, Megiddo and Taanach.

The Hebrew settlers, from their homes on the hillsides, could look down upon this wide plain. They admired the great walled cities. They coveted the well-cared-for vineyards and olive orchards and pasture lands in the broad, green valley. Life on the plain seemed very pleasant and comfortable to the hard-working Hebrews. How much easier it would be to raise big crops down there than it was on the steep hillsides covered with so many rocks and wild bushes and trees, where they were now trying to eke out a bare living!

---

[1] The story in this chapter is found in the Book of Judges. In chapter 4 it is given in prose; in chapter 5 it is given in poetry.

The Powerful Canaanites

If we could have listened to some of these Hebrew settlers in
the twelfth century B.C.E., as they talked together around their
open fires, we might have heard some such remarks as these:

"That land in the plain would make wonderful farms for us
if we could move down there."

"Yes," says another, "but those Canaanites are not like these
in the hill country. We could not possibly capture one of those
walled cities! Much less that whole row of city fortresses!"

"And what is more," says another emphatically, "have you not
heard the rumor that one of the Canaanite kings has appointed
a commander to gather together a big army that is to drive us out
of the land entirely? The great Sisera, with his horses and nine
hundred iron chariots, his spearmen and his archers? What
could we do against such a host?"

"They're already trying to frighten us," says another. "I saw
with my own eyes that refugee family that came to camp below
us last week. I heard them tell how their place had been raided
by a band of these Canaanites from the plain, and that they had
been forced to flee for their lives to the higher hills. It would
not surprise me if those Canaanites started a full-scale attack
soon to drive us all entirely out of the land of Canaan."

"Don't be so gloomy, brother," cries another. "Now is perhaps
not a good time for us to defy these people of the plain, but
someday we shall find a way. The hill country is not enough
for us."

"It is getting to be unsafe for us even to travel the roads near
the valley, for the Canaanites are everywhere," says another.
"One of our caravans bearing food to some of our settlers north
of the plain was attacked last week. All their goods and animals
were carried off and their men made prisoners. I have heard that
no traveler dares to let himself be seen on the roads. They must
make their way along little hidden paths and trails to keep out
of sight of the well-armed Canaanite marauders."

"What do you suppose would happen," another asks thoughtfully, "if Sisera really gathered their armed footmen and their
charioteers against us? But I do not think they could drive their
chariots up here into our hills."

THE PLAIN OF ESDRAELON
A panorama from the summit of Megiddo.

"What troubles me," says still another anxiously, "is that we have no one leader to command all of our people if the Canaanites should attack. Would the men of our brother tribes farther up in the mountains ever come to help those of us who live here near the plain?"

The first speaker, who had started all this excited talk, is now fully roused. "Something must be done," he cries, "and very soon! Someone must gather our forces and attack Sisera before he is able to start his drive against us. But who can do this, and how can we hope to go against these mighty Canaanites in the plain?"

Finally a new voice is heard, speaking with the calm tone of one who does not fully share the fear of his brothers. It is an old man who says: "May it not be that Yahweh will once again come to our aid, as he did in olden times to Moses, and as he has done to our fathers? Is he not a great God, the Lord of hosts, who gives victory to his people? Some of us believe he will help now in our great need. His shrine is at Shiloh and he has his dwelling place at Sinai. But we must believe and hope that he can work some wonderful thing for his people again!"

None of the others tries to speak again, but slowly the group disperses, leaving the old man sitting alone with his thoughts.

A Leader Appears

In another part of the country, as though in answer to the fears and hopes of this troubled group we have been listening to, someone did come forward and try to do something about the danger which threatened the Hebrews. It was not a famed hero of battle—not a seasoned warrior who had proved his valor as a victorious chieftain against the enemy. But it was one whom all the people of the hills knew well, and whom they loved and honored. It was a woman, Deborah, to whom they had long been accustomed to come for counsel. Under an old oak tree,[2] she used to sit and listen to their troubles and settle their quarrels. Like Moses, Deborah had been judging among them.

Now that her people were in trouble, Deborah decided to

---

[2] The Hebrew word in the Bible is translated "palm tree," but scholars think that more likely it was an oak.

take the responsibility for leadership. She sent out a call to all the villages for many miles about, both north and south, east and west, calling for volunteers to help protect them and the land they had won.

Deborah had been told of a young leader of the tribe of Naphtali, named Barak, living to the north. Secretly she sent a messenger to Barak across the Plain of Esdraelon. She called him to gather an army and challenge the forces of Sisera. Carefully Barak made his way across the plain to confer with Deborah.

Deborah laid before him her plan. She said she had seen Yahweh in a vision. "He has commanded us to go forth against Sisera. I do not know how, but somehow, Yahweh will deliver these Canaanites, and their chariots of iron, and their walled cities into our hand."

At first Barak was not so sure he could undertake this fearful task, brave warrior though he was. But he began to count up his resources.

"If you will go with me, Deborah, then I will go," said Barak finally, "but if you will not go with me I will not go."

So, like Joan of Arc in later times, Deborah promised to go into battle. "But," she said to Barak, "do not forget that this undertaking will not be one in which you will win fame for yourself; for it is Yahweh who is going to deliver the mighty Sisera into the hand of a woman!"

When the two were once agreed on their plan, they sent messengers to all the tribes in the hills, both north and south of the Plain of Esdraelon, and even to tribes east of the Jordan, calling for volunteers.

Anxiously they waited for a response. Finally six different tribes sent soldiers to the headquarters in Ephraim, but four tribes failed to send any men at all. Perhaps they were too far away from the scene of battle and felt that, after all, it was not their war, but that of the settlers who lived near the plain. Or it may be that they were too much occupied with their own affairs at home and did not care to go to so much trouble for their neighbors. At any rate, Deborah heaped words of blame upon these shirking stay-at-homes.

The Great Battle of the Plain

It was a wild horde that finally gathered, some armed perhaps with bows and arrows, others with clubs and sling shots. But what odds there were against these warriors from the hills! A well-trained Canaanite army, fully equipped with spears and swords, a force probably twice the size of the army from the hills! With nine hundred prancing war horses and heavy chariots besides! A fearful foe to meet! What was most perilous of all for the forces of Deborah and Barak was that the battle had to be joined down on the plain, where the wilder mountain-dwelling tribes were less able to fight, but where the Canaanites would be able to maneuver their troops and chariots to best advantage.

Undaunted by the immense difficulties facing them, Deborah and Barak and their armies went bravely forward; for did they not believe they had been called in the name of Yahweh, their God? Was it not his battle, as well as theirs, which they must fight? They would trust their war God to help them win!

Rumor of the Hebrew uprising reached the camp of Sisera. From the west came his great army toward the city of Taanach near the banks of the River Kishon. Horsemen and chariots dashed across the small stream, confident of victory over that mob of wild, angry farmers waiting dully on the strip of plain between them and the low hills beyond. Surely there was nothing for the Hebrews to do but to break ranks and run to the hills for shelter!

But a dark storm cloud had been gathering over the mountains to the east. It came sweeping down above the valley over the heads of the two armies. To the Canaanites, the huge, black, threatening mass in the heavens was a fearful thing. It seemed as though the whole darkness of night had gathered itself into one body and was about to fling itself upon them. Coming, as it did, from behind the Hebrews, they saw the cloud only as it moved over the heads of their enemies and then burst in fury upon them. To the Hebrews, it seemed like the sudden appearance of a mighty reinforcing army coming to help them. Could it be Yahweh, arriving from his distant home on the sacred mountain of Sinai in the south?

Peals of thunder echoed through the hills, and a blazing flash

CANAANITE CHARIOTEERS IN BATTLE
An ivory plaque from Megiddo.

of lightning seemed to split the cloud wide open as it hung over the heads of the Canaanites who now stood still in horror. Down came the rain like a savage flood. "Yahweh has come in the storm cloud to help us!" shouted the Hebrews. The ground was turned into a sea of mud beneath the feet of the Canaanites. Their clothes and their weapons were soaked, their eyes blinded. They thrashed about helplessly while their horses leaped and bucked frantically. The chariot wheels bogged down. Sisera's mighty army soon broke into a disorderly mob. Each man was bent only upon trying to save himself. All together, they turned about, intending to go back across the Kishon River; but it was no longer the little, peaceful stream they had crossed a short while before. In its place, a raging torrent was pouring fiercely down and rushing out over its banks.

The whole scene had changed in but a few moments. Deborah sounded the trumpet call for a charge. The shouting crowds of Hebrew tribesmen, caring not for mud or rain, bore down upon the floundering, ruined troops of Sisera. The strong, proud Canaanite enemy was being beaten, and was fleeing in terror, with Barak and his men in hot pursuit. So sudden and heaven-sent did the defeat seem that some actually believed that even the stars in the sky had used their influence to send down the pouring rain to flood the River Kishon. In the song of victory which the Hebrews afterwards sang, they put it this way:

> From heaven fought the stars,
> From their courses the stars fought against Sisera.

Seeing his forces broken and fleeing, the great Sisera also

abandoned his chariot and ran for safety. Finally he found shelter in the tent of a Kenite woman, Jael, who lived not far from the battlefield. While pretending to be his friend, this woman was really on the Hebrews' side. She invited Sisera to lie down to rest. She brought him a bowl of milk. But even as he sat up to drink it, Jael struck his head from behind with a hammer. No greater disgrace could be imagined for a great warrior, leading his army gloriously into battle, than to meet his end at the hands of a defenseless woman!

For centuries the Hebrews sang of this important victory. It served to draw together at least six of the Hebrew tribes in loyalty to one another and to Yahweh, their God. They believed that Yahweh had actually come down from the sky to help them in their desperate need. They were firmly convinced that Yahweh had wanted them, his "chosen people," to possess the plains as well as the hills of Canaan. Only by wresting the plains from the control of the Canaanites could passes through the hills and the caravan roads be kept safe from enemies' attacks.

With this conquest, the Hebrews must have come into possession of some of the important walled cities of the plain. Of these, Megiddo was the greatest stronghold. From recent excavations, it is known that this fortress came into the hands of the Hebrews about this time and remained theirs for a number of centuries. Megiddo stood on a high point of rock which overlooked several great highways that met at that place. Along these roads all approaching armies had to march.

The Ancient Song of Deborah

The oldest ballad in the Bible is the song celebrating this victory. It is usually called "The Song of Deborah" and is found in the fifth chapter of the Book of Judges. It is thought that this poem must have been written shortly after the battle, either by one who participated in it, or by one who was a contemporary, because so vivid and direct is its picture of that dramatic scene. It probably can be dated about 1150 B.C.E.

It is a grim and cruel story, as all wars are grim and cruel. Whether one takes sides with the Canaanites or with the Hebrews, it is shocking to hear the praise of Jael's treacherous murder of the great Sisera and to find the writer taking such gloating pleasure in the sorrow of Sisera's aged mother, waiting in vain for his return. One wonders also when mankind will ever free itself from a belief in a god who lends his supernatural powers to help one army against another! [3]

Because the leaders took the lead in Israel,
    Because the people freely volunteered,
Praise Yahweh!
Hear, O you kings; you princes, listen!
    I will sing to Yahweh,
I will sing praise to Yahweh, the God of Israel.
Yahweh, when thou wentest forth from Seir,
    When thou didst march from the land of Edom,
The earth trembled, the heavens also dropped,
    Yea, the clouds dropped water.
The mountains quaked before Yahweh,
    Even the One from Sinai,
Before Yahweh, the God of Israel!

Praise Yahweh!
You that ride on brown donkeys,
    You that sit on rich carpets,
And you that walk by the way—sing!
    Hear the loud cheers at the watering-places!
There they recount the victories of Yahweh,
    The victories of his peasants in Israel,
How the people of Yahweh went down to battle.

Awake! Awake, Deborah!
    Awake and strike up the song!
Arise, Barak, and seize your captives,
    O son of Ahinoam!

Then came down only a remnant of the nobles,
    The people of Yahweh came down as heroes!
From Ephraim they rushed forth into the valley,
    After him Benjamin, among your people;
From Machir (Manasseh) came down commanders,
    And from Zebulon those who carry the marshal's staff.
And the princes of Issachar were with Deborah;
    As was Issachar so was Barak—
Into the valley he rushed among his foot soldiers.

[3] The prose account of this battle given in the fourth chapter of Judges is thought to have been written later than the poem.

Among the clans of Reuben, great were the heart-searchings.
  Why did you sit among the sheepfolds,
Listening to the pipings for the flocks?
  Gilead remained beyond the Jordan;
And Dan, why did he stay by the ships as an alien?
  Asher sat still by the shore of the sea
And remained by its landing places.
Zebulum was a people that risked their lives to the death,
  And Naphthali, too, on the heights of the field.
The kings came and fought;
  Then fought the kings of Canaan,
At Taanach by the waters of Megiddo;
  But they took no booty of silver.
From heaven fought the stars,
  From their courses they fought against Sisera.
The River Kishon swept them away,
The ancient river, the River Kishon.
Blessed above all women shall Jael be,
  Most blessed of all women who live in tents.
He asked water, and she gave him milk,
  She brought him rich, buttery curds in a lordly bowl.
Then she put her hand to the tent-pin,
  And her right hand to the workman's hammer;
With the hammer she battered Sisera, she crushed his head;
  Yea, she pierced and struck through his temple.
At her feet he sank down, he fell, he lay still,
  Where he sank, there he lay slain.
By the window leaned Sisera's mother,
  She looked through the lattice and cried:
Why is his chariot so long in coming?
  Why tarry the hoof-beats of his horses?
The wisest of her princesses answered her,
  Yea, 'twas she that made reply to her:
Are they not finding, dividing the spoil?
  A maiden or two for each man;
Booty of dyed garments for Sisera,
  Booty of richly embroidered garments,
Yes, two pieces of embroidered stuff.
So let all Thine enemies perish, O Yahweh,
  But let them that love Thee be as the sun
  When he rises in his might.

5

Gideon, Champion of the Central Tribes

THE PEOPLE OF THE SIX DIFFERENT TRIBES that had rallied to the battle call of Deborah and Barak returned to their own separate settlements, each hoping to be able to live in peace. Now that this danger from Sisera's chariots had been successfully overcome, each tribe became absorbed in its own problems of living. There was no thought as yet of a union of all the Hebrew tribes to form a single nation in the new land. At this time, the different tribes lived together only as neighbors in the same country, and not always were they even friendly neighbors. They sometimes fought each other, and if an enemy threatened one or another of the tribes, that tribe might have to defend itself single-handed, with no help from the other tribes.[1]

These Hebrew farmers on the hills were never wholly free from danger for very long, even when the Canaanites were not actively hostile. Other roving bands from the deserts east of the Jordan were always hovering about the edges of the cultivated districts, ready to make raids upon the settlers. They would steal their grain as soon as it was harvested or they would carry off animals from the flocks and herds. Most of these marauders had no thought of settling down in the land as the Hebrews had done. They would merely move in stealthily like wild animals after their prey, pounce upon their victims, seize food and steal any booty they could lay hold of, and then slink away again into the deserts across the Jordan.

The Hebrews of the tribe of Manasseh who lived in the hill country near the upper Jordan were troubled by just such plunderers. These were camel-driving nomads, called Midianites. They poured into the country from the desert lands south and

---

[1] The stories in this chapter are found in Judges 6: 2-6, 11-24, 36-40; 7: 1-24; 8: 12-32.

east of the Jordan. They entered Canaan through the far eastern end of the Plain of Esdraelon, usually called the Plain of Jezreel. There they pitched their tents and camped with their women and children, and with their camels and sheep. From this safe base, they sent forth their fighting bands, to raid the fields and villages on the hills. Sometimes these marauders attacked those who lived south of the great valley, and sometimes they attacked the tribes on the north side.

So numerous were the Midianite bands, and so great was the damage they did, that they seemed like swarms of locusts swooping down on the fields to eat up all the grass and grain, leaving the farms stripped to the ground. No one knew just when the Midianites might come, but it was usually when the harvest had just been reaped. The farmers would have barely gathered in their crops, joyfully anticipating the abundant provisions they now had for the winter ahead, when—alas!—all their hopes would be dashed to the ground by the arrival of these hordes of human vultures from the desert.

Season after season, for a number of years, the Hebrews of the tribe of Manasseh had endured this plundering of their crops. The settlers who lived nearest the desert, where the Midianites entered their territory, had lost the most. Many had been forced to leave their village homes and to flee to the mountains. There they built rude shelters in the woods or fortified themselves in caves and in the dens of animals. If these plundering nomads were ever to be stopped, some leader must be found who could organize the poor, distressed farmers to rise against their enemies and save themselves.

Their Champion Is Aroused

Apparently the tribe of Manasseh had no one strong chief who ruled the entire tribe. Each clan lived its own life in its own village, quite apart from the rest. Now there was in the village of Ophrah, however, a chieftain named Joash who had several sons, one of whom was familiarly called Gideon.

The wheat had just been harvested. It was important that it be threshed and stored away quickly where no thieves could find it. Gideon did not dare to thresh the grain on the hilltop where he usually worked. Instead he hid himself in the hollow stone-

CANAAN BEFORE THE HEBREW INVASION
The cities are indicated by both their old and their modern names.

lined place in the hill which they ordinarily used as a wine press. Beating out the grains of wheat from the chaff in such a place where the wind did not blow was hard work, but Gideon was desperate.

All the while, as he beat the wheat stalks, he kept his eye open for the possible approach of raiders. He was thinking bitter thoughts. "Something must be done to rid the countryside of these murderers!" He looked up over the edge of the wine press to make sure he was alone, but to his great surprise he saw a man sitting near-by under a tree, looking at him! Gideon was frightened. Was this a Midianite leader coming ahead of the band to warn him that it would be useless to try to resist? But the man began speaking softly to Gideon. "Yahweh is with you, O brave man!" he said.

"Oh, my lord, if Yahweh is with us, why has all this trouble come to us?" Gideon's voice shook from the sudden fear that had seized him. "And where are all Yahweh's wonderful deeds, such as our fathers tell us about when they say, 'Did not Yahweh bring our ancestors out of Egypt?' But now it seems that Yahweh has abandoned us and has put us into the hands of these marauding Midianites!"

"You must go with your great strength to save Israel from the Midianites. I am sending you!" the visitor replied.

Gideon, astonished at the man's words, looked earnestly at his visitor, wondering what to say. Feeling his own helplessness in the face of this swarm of Midianites, he finally found his voice and said: "Oh, my lord, how can I ever save Israel? My family is the poorest in the Manasseh tribe, and I am really the weakest of all my father's sons." But the stranger insisted: "Surely, Yahweh will be with you, and you will overcome and drive away these Midianites as though they were only one man."

As the man spoke these words, Gideon looked off over the hills that stretched away in the distance. He thought of all his people of the tribe of Manasseh, who must be saved from the desolating attacks of the Midianites. He looked again at the man before him. The steady, clear eyes of the visitor, and the calm voice in which he had spoken, made Gideon feel that he must rise to this challenge and rally his people against the plundering Midianites.

But when the stranger had gone, Gideon began to wonder.

Had he been dreaming, or had he really seen and talked with this stranger? Who was he? One of the ancient storytellers later declared that Gideon's visitor was none other than a messenger (an "angel") of Yahweh, and that when Gideon gratefully served his guest some food, the stranger touched it with the end of his staff instead of eating it. At once it burst into flame as though it were an offering being sacrificed to Yahweh. Then, it is said, Gideon built an altar to Yahweh and gave it the name "Yahweh-Shalom," meaning "Yahweh is Peace," feeling that he and his people would now be kept safe by the God of Israel.

"Gideon's Fleece"

Whatever may have happened, Gideon was apparently still uncertain. One of his later admirers tells another story to show how Gideon struggled in his own mind before he acted. To us who live in a scientific age, these stories seem strange. To understand them, we must appreciate how differently people thought in those ancient times from the way educated people think today. In Gideon's time, it was commonly believed, for example, that a god might indicate what he wanted a person to do by making something very unusual happen to him. The story says that Gideon wanted this kind of "sign." Some today may say that Gideon was asking for "magic," but if we use that word "magic" for the thing Gideon wanted, we should know that Gideon was not looking for anything in the nature of a trick. It was a *real* happening that he wanted, something that he believed no human being alone could do. Gideon wanted a "miracle," a supernatural happening brought about by a supernatural being, who, he believed, could do anything.

In this case, according to the ancient story, Gideon even told the God exactly the kind of "miracle" he wanted. In the evening, he spread a sheepskin (a fleece) on the ground, asking the God, Yahweh, to cause dew to come on the fleece, but *only* on the fleece and not on the ground. Curiously enough, this is just what is said to have happened. In fact, the story says that when Gideon arose the next morning he actually squeezed out a whole bowlful of water from the fleece, while there was not a drop of dew on the ground around it! But to make doubly sure of Yahweh's intention to have him lead the attack, Gideon asked that on the next night the sign should be reversed: that the fleece should be left entirely dry while the ground around it should be covered with dew. And the next morning, it is said, he found it was even as he had asked.

Whatever may have happened, Gideon was finally assured that he was the man to lead an attack against the Midianites. He went all through the region where his clansmen lived. By the blowing of his trumpet he gathered the villagers together. He called for volunteers to join in ridding the country of these plunderers and murderers. He sent his messengers to other villages farther off, and to other tribes, calling them also to come and help. "For the sword of Yahweh and of Gideon!" was his call to battle. He sent messengers even across the plain, to the tribe of Naphtali farther north on the shores of the Sea of Galilee, to call their fighting men to follow him. Thousands of men rallied about him, camping on the slopes of Mount Gilboa, ready to fight.

"Gideon's Three Hundred"

Gideon was a man of cunning. He realized that more could be gained by careful planning than by mere strength and numbers of men. He must trick his foes by a night attack. He must frighten them suddenly by some kind of deceit. For these purposes, a few daring men who could be trusted to keep their heads in a crisis, and who would be able to act quickly under orders, would be worth far more than an army of thousands. Yet the larger numbers would be useful later on when perhaps the enemy would be trying to escape.

First of all, then, Gideon needed to plan a way by which he could pick out, from the thousands who had been mustered, only the bravest and most capable soldiers. To make a successful surprise attack on the enemies' camp would call for extraordinary bravery and quickness of action. This, therefore, is what Gideon did. He ordered that all who were already frightened, or who found themselves trembling, should go back to their homes for the time being. The result? Two out of every three men went home, leaving only ten thousand men to go to battle!

Still Gideon was not satisfied. Ten thousand men were too many for a night attack. What then did he do? He led these ten thousand down to the edge of a near-by stream and told them to drink. Gideon watched closely as they did this. He saw that some of them kneeled down beside the stream and put their faces down into the water in order to suck it up into their mouths. Others stepped right out into the stream and merely stooped and carried the water to their mouths with their cupped hands.

What was it Gideon was after in this strange test? It is said he chose the three hundred men who merely stooped and scooped the water up into their cupped hands, because even while they drank they would be able to keep watch, and be prepared in an instant for a surprise attack of the enemy. The others who stooped to kneel and who put their faces down into the water would be caught completely off guard if an enemy should suddenly appear. Gideon was testing their quickness of action and their alertness.

As the story of Gideon's further moves is told in the Bible, the impression is given that all these brilliant plans for a surprise attack were dictated to Gideon by the God, Yahweh, and that what Gideon did was merely to do as Yahweh commanded. Indeed, the writer definitely states that it all happened in this way so that the praise for the victory would not be taken by Gideon or by his men, but be given to Yahweh alone.

A Third Sign—An Overheard Dream

Whether or not this ancient story, as it is told in the Bible, gives us the true details, it seems that only a small, picked number of men shared in Gideon's night attack on the Midianite camp. Having cleverly thought through his plans, the next step was to decide when to make the attack. To answer this question, Gideon had still more investigating to do.

In the darkness of night, taking with him but one trusted servant, Gideon crept cautiously up to the edge of the enemies' camp to see what he might learn about their strength or weakness. How well guarded was the camp? How could they be frightened? As Gideon and his companion approached the enemies' lines, they heard talking. Two sentries on guard were whiling away the long night hours, and keeping each other awake by exchanging stories. Gideon strained his ears in the darkness to hear what they were saying. One sentry was telling the other: "Last night I had a dream. I saw a huge loaf of barley bread come tumbling into our camp, and as it rolled along it struck my tent—or was it the general's tent?—and turned it over. What do you suppose that dream means?"

Gideon and his servant listened sharply to what the second sentry would say. There was silence for several minutes before the answer came. "I believe that loaf of barley bread means that these Hebrew farmers, who raise barley on their farms, are going to fall upon us suddenly and bring confusion to our camp. We are certainly not ready for a surprise attack. I'm afraid your dream means that Gideon and his army are going to defeat us!"

What Gideon heard was enough for him. Now he knew that at least some of the Midianites were afraid of the coming battle. In that case the battle was already half won, for when men are frightened by what lies ahead, they are already half defeated.

A Clever Night Attack

Now Gideon was convinced. That very night was the time to attack. He believed Yahweh was commanding him to act. Stealthily Gideon and his servant returned to their own camp. Gideon wakened his men. He divided them into three companies and instructed them in what they were to do.

"Watch me," he said, "and do what you see me do." He produced an earthenware pitcher, and a lighted torch or firebrand. He thrust the torch into the pitcher so that its light could not be seen. Then he gave a shout, broke the pitcher on the ground, and the light blazed forth. "Do that," he said, "when I give the signal."

Each man was then given a pitcher and a torch. "Now," continued Gideon, "when you reach the outposts of the Midianite camp, one company of you will defile to the right, one to the left, and I will lead the central company straight toward the enemy camp. The Midianites will think they are surrounded. Are we ready?"

Under cover of night, the three companies climbed down the hillside to the plain. They were as silent as the night itself. As they approached the great camp in the valley, it was nearly midnight. They could hear the change of sentries taking place. Little did these sentries, or the sleeping hosts of the Midianites

AN UNKNOWN HEBREW

*An ancient bas-relief found on a temple wall
at Karnak in Egypt.*

whom they were meant to guard, know what lay in store for them during the next few minutes!

Suddenly a trumpet sounded—Gideon's signal—and the still night was shattered by an unearthly noise. The black darkness was aglow with flaring lights all around the Midianite camp. A deafening cry sounded through the valley: "For the sword of Yahweh and of Gideon!"—as though thousands of men were shouting the battle cry.

Taken completely off guard, the Midianites' first thought was that the army of the Hebrews was upon them in full force, and panic seized them. They sprang up and ran, not knowing where to go in the darkness and confusion. They bumped and tramped one another in their haste to escape. In their fright they mistook friend for foe, and though Gideon's men did not move from their places as they kept shouting the battle cry and waving their torches, the terrified, stampeding Midianites thought they were being pursued and turned their weapons on one another. Those who could get away fled in the one direction open to them, toward the Jordan River and toward their homes east of the river. Routed and scattered, running pell-mell, they left all their possessions behind, bent only on escape from the fearful foe in the darkness of night.

Gideon now commanded his men to take up the pursuit of the wild mob, and to follow them toward the Jordan. The next morning they were joined by many of those Hebrew soldiers who had earlier been dismissed from Gideon's army, but who had lingered near to watch the battle. Gideon sent a messenger ahead to the people of the Ephraim tribe that lived along the Jordan, calling upon them to cut off the enemies' retreat by guarding the fords of the river. There the fugitives were halted temporarily, though some of them succeeded in crossing the river. But in a short time Gideon's men caught up with the main body of fleeing Midianites and took two of their kings captive.

On Gideon's victorious return to his home in Ophrah, it is said that a great crowd gathered together and demanded that he become their king. Although Gideon refused to be called a king, he did become their chief and their priest.

"I have one request to make of you," he said that afternoon. "Bring me all the golden ear-rings and nose-rings that you took from the Midianites. Bring also the golden chains and crescents you took from the necks of their camels, and I will make for you an *ephod*. And we will build a shrine for the *ephod* so that there may be a place where you may come to inquire of Yahweh whenever you feel the need of help."

So Gideon had a large cloth spread out on the ground, and the people gladly brought their golden ornaments and threw them onto the cloth until there were many pounds of golden ornaments. Then Gideon commanded a skilled workman to make an *ephod*. Perhaps it was somewhat like the ark that the Hebrews under Moses had carried with them through the desert. A goldsmith overlaid and ornamented the box with the gold. Perhaps he found some stones cut or scratched with peculiar marks and placed them in the *ephod*.

Gideon had a shrine built, and he placed the golden *ephod* in the shrine. From then on, whenever a person wished to come to Gideon with a question or a problem he did not know how to answer, Gideon would go alone into the shrine. He would speak to Yahweh and ask what was the right thing to do. Then Gideon would close his eyes and open the *ephod* and put his hand in and bring out one or more of the stones. And from the markings on the particular stone he had taken, he would read Yahweh's answer.

Exactly what this ancient way of praying was like, we do not know, but we do know that it was some kind of casting of lots at a sacred shrine, and for the Hebrews a shrine was a house where Yahweh was thought surely to be.

Gideon lived to a ripe old age, and as long as he lived his people were never again troubled by the Midianites. Gideon married a number of wives and he had many sons. Both wives and sons were thought to be signs of Yahweh's special favor.

So great did his people consider Gideon's victory over the Midianites that long afterward it ranked as one of the mighty acts of Yahweh for his people. Songs were sung to celebrate the victory. It was called "The Day of Midian." The eighty-third Psalm is one of these songs of victory that the people used to sing when they gathered around their campfires in the evening to dance and be glad.

6

Samson, Champion of the Tribe of Dan

A New Danger Arises

Now that the Midianites from the eastern desert had been successfully overcome and driven out, it would seem that the Hebrew settlers might enjoy a time of peace. This was the case with the tribes settled in the central and eastern part of the land who now were secure in their homes in the hills. But for the tribe of Dan, in the west, whose territory reached down toward the plain which skirted the Mediterranean shore, a new danger arose.[1]

This new threat came from another invading group, called the Philistines. While the Hebrews had been working their way into Canaan from the east, these Philistines had been entering the country from the Mediterranean Sea. These Philistines were not just raiders, like the Midianites, who attacked the earlier settlers, plundered their homes and farms and then retreated with the booty to their own homes. No, these other invaders, like the Hebrews themselves, were planning to conquer the whole of Canaan and to make it their homeland.

What was even more disturbing, these Philistines were not just simple shepherds accustomed to roving over the desert. They were a highly civilized and skillful people. Some think they came from the Island of Crete because so many vases with Cretan designs have been found in the ruins of their homes. These Philistines were also skilled seamen and traders. By this time, they had already built and occupied five good-sized walled cities along the coastal plain. The Philistines were strong, large men, well trained in warfare. They had their horses and chariots.

---

[1] The stories in this chapter are found in the Book of Judges, chapter 16, verses 4-30.

They knew how to make sharp swords and spears of iron. They wore armor and carried shields of brass when they fought.

The time had now come when these Philistines decided to take over more of the country. So they began attacking the little settlements of the Hebrews nestling on the low hills farther to the east and north of them. These villages belonged to the tribe of Dan, and their people were afraid of the powerful Philistines. Instead of fighting back, the Danites began to withdraw from their villages and to move farther into the highlands. This was very discouraging.

Years after, as the Hebrews looked back on these dark days, they told stories of the brave and strong among them who had refused to give up. One of these champions was named Samson. Because the people needed so badly to keep up their courage, they wanted to hear these stories of Samson over and over. If his exploits grew with the telling, it did not matter to the listeners. They were ready to believe almost anything. These stories, as they were finally put down in writing, resemble the feats told of Paul Bunyan, the superman of American pioneer days. Whether a Samson ever really lived, no one can say. Nor, if he did live, can any one say how many of these deeds of wonder he actually performed.

The Storyteller Begins

Let us imagine ourselves living in a hillside village and sitting down one evening with our neighbors in an open place among the houses, where we listen to a storyteller of long ago.

Dusk is settling over the village. The scene is lighted only by a great bonfire around which the people sit on the ground. All is quiet as the assembled villagers wait expectantly to hear of the fame and the mighty deeds of one of their heroes of olden times, who had outwitted the enemy of their people many times.

The speaker stands near the fire so that all can see him plainly. He begins: "Hear, O ye sons of Israel, and I will tell you the story of the renowned Samson, of the tribe of Dan, and how he confounded the mighty Philistines and put fear into their hearts.

"You have heard, O my countrymen, of the heroes of old: of Deborah and Barak, who put Sisera and his hosts to flight in the

Plain of Esdraelon; of Gideon, who chased away the wild, plundering Midianites and drove them back to their desert tents. These all led forth the armies of our people against our foes. But now I shall tell you of another champion, Samson, the wonder man of Zorah in the Valley of Sorek. No armies followed him. No warriors rose up with him to fight on fields of battle. By his own cunning and feats of strength, single-handed, he brought dismay to the proud Philistines.

"The Philistines could not understand the secret of Samson's great strength. Among us, his own people, it was commonly believed that Samson had this great strength because he had never shaved his beard or cut his hair. Samson himself believed that. He used to say, 'A divine power lives in the hair and when the hair is cut off this divine power is taken away.' Whatever the reason was, my friends, we know that the spirit of our God Yahweh was in Samson—the spirit of the God who can throw thunderbolts from the sky, the spirit of the God who can send hailstorms and floods and earthquakes. This was the mighty spirit that lived in Samson.[2]

"I have often told you of the great things Samson could do. Once he killed a lion with his bare hands, and tore it apart as though it was nothing but a newborn lamb or a young goat. He could slay a thousand men with no weapon but the jawbone of a donkey. He could tear loose the massive gates of a walled city, with their great posts and lock-bars, and carry them away on his back to the top of a mountain forty miles away! Try as they would, the Philistines could not capture Samson or keep him from troubling them."

Delilah Plays a Game With Her Lover

"Now there lived in the valley of Sorek a very charming woman, named Delilah. One day as Samson was out on one of his adventures, he met this beautiful woman and at once fell in love with her. Even though she was not one of his own people, Samson made up his mind he was going to marry her. He was so eager he did not take time to find out the kind of person she really was. He did not know that she had been making friends

---

[2] This belief that a special divine power resides in the hair is a primitive belief that has been held by a number of different races.

A Loom Like Delilah's
A modern Jew weaves on the same kind of loom used 3000 years ago.

with the leading Philistines in the valley. Samson thought Delilah loved him as much as he loved her.

"When her Philistine friends heard how Delilah had won the heart of this Hebrew giant, five of them went to her secretly to persuade her to help them capture him. 'We want this man in our power. Trick him into telling you what is the secret of his great strength, for he has troubled us these many years. We will pay you well. See, each one of us has here eleven hundred pieces of silver to give you if you will do this for us.' The money was enticing to Delilah. She was flattered by the prospect of showing her own great power.

"Soon after that, as she was talking with her lover one day, she asked him, just as a child might ask her father: 'Tell me, Samson, how can you be so wonderfully strong?· Could anyone ever bind you so that you could not get loose?'

" 'Shall I tell you?' said Samson, not suspecting the reason for her question. He paused to think what he would say, and then playfully told her: 'If you would bind my arms with seven green, braided willow twigs that have not been dried, then I would be helpless, no stronger than any other man.' The next day Delilah told this to her five Philistine friends. At once they gathered some tough green thongs and brought them to Delilah. They said: 'Tonight we will hide ourselves nearby, when Samson comes to see you. When you have bound him, call for us.'

"Idly Delilah fingered the willow twigs as she talked with Samson. Finally she said: 'Samson, let me bind your arms with these, just for fun.' Samson, falling in with what he thought was her joking mood, consented, and in a moment she had wound the braided twigs about his arms, tying them securely. When she saw him thus, apparently helpless before her, she suddenly cried out with a laugh: 'Samson, the Philistines are here to take you!' But before they could come, even before Samson saw them or knew that they were really there, he broke the shackles as easily as one might burn through a piece of string with a flame.

"Delilah pouted and said: 'Samson, you have fooled me. You have told me a lie. Tell me now, how can you really be bound so that you cannot get loose?'

"Still not suspecting her purpose, Samson thought he would

carry on the little game with her, so he said: 'If you take brand-new ropes that have never been used, and tie my arms with them, I shall not be able to move.' Again Delilah did as he told her, binding him this time with new ropes which the Philistines had secretly brought to her. Seeing him bound, Delilah cried out, as before: 'The Philistines are here, Samson!' But the Philistines could not come near before Samson gave a mighty heave of his arms and snapped the ropes as though they were threads.

"Disappointed, Delilah tried again the next evening to coax him, determined to find out how she might make him completely helpless. 'What a big, strong man you are!' she said flatteringly. 'I don't think there is anything that can bind your powerful arms, is there? You've just been deceiving me all this time. Tell me, what is strong enough to hold you so that you cannot break loose?' Even this third time, Samson was not suspicious of her purpose, for he thought Delilah's shouts about the Philistines were just a part of the fun. He had not caught sight of them lurking near-by the other times. So he thought he would play still another trick of the same kind.

" 'If you weave my long hair in with the strong cords in that loom over there, then I shall not be able to break loose,' he told her. This time Delilah said nothing about it for several days, waiting meanwhile for a chance to bind him in this new way. One day when he came in from a long day of walking in the country, she sat with him in a corner near the loom. As the evening wore away, Samson became drowsy, as she had hoped he would, and soon he was napping with his head leaning against the loom. Softly she stood up, took hold of his long waving locks of hair and twined them into the web of the loom. As soon as she had finished, she again cried out: 'The Philistines are here, Samson!' Samson leaped up, suddenly wide awake, and tore himself from the web, again before the hiding Philistines could show themselves.

"Delilah, now thoroughly angry with him, said peevishly: 'How can you say that you love me, when you go on playing tricks upon me three times over!'

"By this time Samson, too, was beginning to grow tired of her constant teasing, for she had kept on asking him the same question again and again: 'Tell me truly, dear Samson,' she begged. 'Tell me the secret of your great strength.' Finally he decided to tell her the truth and to stop his jesting. He did not want her to think that he did not love her. 'I'll tell you the real secret this time, Delilah,' he said. 'It is because of my long hair that I am so strong. As a child I was taught never to allow my hair to be cut. By keeping my hair long, I believe I have kept more of the power of our God Yahweh than other men have. If my hair were to be cut off I should become weak, and be as any other man.'

"This time Delilah was sure that he had told her the whole truth. She therefore sent a message secretly to the Philistine leaders: 'Come to me just this once more, for he has told me the secret at last.' They came at once, bringing with them the money for her reward, and hiding themselves near-by to be ready at her signal. Again she took the opportunity when Samson, tired from his day in the open, was drowsing as he visited her. When at last he fell asleep, Delilah called a man to come in and cut off Samson's hair. When the barber had finished his work, Delilah cried out: 'The Philistines are here to take you Samson!' He sprang up, not knowing what had been done; only half awake, he said to himself: 'I'll shake myself free as I have always done,' for he dreamily thought Delilah had only bound him as she had done before. But this time, to his grief, he suddenly felt his weakness.

"Quickly the Philistines came out of their hiding place, seized him and dragged him off to prison. There they cruelly put out his eyes, as the ancients often did with prisoners whom they feared. Poor Samson! To make matters even worse, they took him down to Gaza, the very Philistine city whose heavy gates Samson had once playfully carried away! And there they bound him with brass chains and set him to work pulling heavy mill-stones around and around to grind grain. The usual work of a donkey or camel!

"But this was not yet the end of Samson! As he toiled away day after day and week after week, his hair began to grow again and his strength was returning. He did not realize this, nor did his persecutors."

The Great Sacrifice in the Temple

"A day came when the Philistines were planning to hold a thanksgiving festival in the temple to their God, whom they called Dagon. A great sacrifice was to be offered to the God, in order to show the people's thankfulness. Someone suggested: 'Why not bring out Samson and offer him as our sacrifice? For Dagon, our God, has put him into our hands!' So when the feast was at its height, the cry was heard, passing from lip to lip among the crowds of people: 'Bring out Samson! Bring out Samson!' And someone said: 'Let's make sport of him before he is sacrificed. He has destroyed so many of our people with his clever tricks!' 'Yes,' shouted others, 'let him show us some of his foolish pranks now!'

"So they sent for Samson, and a young boy led him by the

A PHILISTINE ALTAR OF INCENSE
With Cretan painted designs.

hand out of his prison. The crowd jeered when they saw the once strong man, now helpless, blind, and chained, led along by the little lad.

"As Samson shuffled along beside the boy, holding on to his hand as he moved through the inky blackness of his blindness, they came to the temple of Dagon where the great crowd of the Philistines had gathered. Samson could hear the noise and shouting coming from the wide-open court around which the flat-roofed buildings were grouped. Behind him he could hear the jeers of the people who packed the building on whose porch he was standing. He turned to the boy beside him and said: 'Lead me to the pillars that support this temple, so that I may lean on them!'

"As Samson stood there helpless in his darkness, he whispered a prayer of vengeance upon his tormentors: 'O Yahweh, my God, give me back all my vanished strength just this once to get revenge on these Philistines for my two eyes.' With this he placed his hand against the two main pillars that supported the great building, and he pushed with all his might. As he did so he cried: 'Let me die with these Philistines!'

"With a terrific crash, down came the pillars and roof of the temple, burying Samson and all the occupants of the building beneath the ruins. Hundreds of the others sitting on the roof were hurled to their death, while the falling walls killed hundreds more who had been standing in the courtyard before the temple. So the Philistines who died with Samson were more in number than those he had killed during all his life!"

The Storyteller Ends His Tale

So the tragic story ends. The villagers, among whom we have been sitting, were listening with bated breath. Now for a few moments they remain in silence. Then some one begins wailing a chant. "The Philistines who died with Samson were more in number than all those he killed in all his life!" Others take up the mournful dirge. Over and over they chant it. The moaning rises to a crescendo and then dies away, as the fire burns low and the darkness deepens.

7

A Losing Struggle

The Philistine Threat Grows

When the Hebrews retreated, the Philistines were merely encouraged to push farther inland. More villages on the hillsides, both to the north and to the south, were occupied by the Philistines, and more Hebrews were killed or made the slaves of their conquerors.[1]

Large numbers of Philistines moved up into the valley of Sharon. They made war against one clan after another, often gaining important victories. How long could the Hebrews survive the attacks of this well-armed enemy? How long would they be able to live in the land of Canaan at all? The situation was growing desperate.

The "elders" or older men of several tribes in the region got together. They called the young men of their villages to rise up and fight—or else they and their families would all be driven from the land. Many young men volunteered. An army was hurriedly gathered and went forth to meet the Philistines, and the Philistines marched forth to meet the Hebrews. The two armies were joined in battle somewhere on the Plain of Sharon. There the Philistines used their chariots and horses to good advantage. They overwhelmed the poorly armed and untrained Hebrew army and slew several thousand men.

A few survivors of the Hebrews straggled back to their camp, greatly discouraged. They talked over their bitter experience. The elders, too, were heavy-hearted. "Why has Yahweh allowed us to be so badly beaten?" was all they could say. Yet even as they said this, they did not give up their determination to try once more to defend their homes against the Philistines' attacks. They must not give up after one defeat. But what could they do?

---

[1] The stories in this chapter are found in the I Samuel, chapters 4, 5, 6; and in the first four verses of chapter 7.

A Desperate Plan Is Tried

Finally one of the elders spoke up. "I know what we must do," he said. "We must bring the ark of Yahweh from Shiloh to lead us into battle. Do you not remember how our fathers won their victories when they carried the ark before them against their enemies? Do you not remember how Yahweh went with Moses and his people when they carried the ark with them? We shall do well if we bring the ark from its resting place in Shiloh." The other elders agreed, and it was decided to carry the ark with them into their next battle against the Philistines.

When messengers were sent to the temple in Shiloh, however, it was not easy to persuade Eli, the aged priest, to let the ark be taken away. "What shall we do here," he asked, "if you remove the ark from its place? When the people come to bring their questions to Yahweh, what can I say to them if Yahweh has departed?" But the matter was urgent. The elders and the fighting men desperately needed to feel that Yahweh was with them in their struggle to overcome the Philistines.

Finally Eli yielded. But he insisted on sending his two sons with the ark, to watch over it and to represent him as its guardians, for he was anxious lest some disaster might come to the ark if it were taken away from its accustomed place in the temple of Shiloh.

Standing at the door of the temple, Eli watched his two sons carry the precious ark between them on their shoulders, down the steps and away. When they and the soldiers following them were all beyond sight, Eli turned around sadly and walked back into the temple court, and over toward the curtained room where the sacred ark had always stood in the darkness. As Eli stood there in silence before the empty room, he felt a fearsome loneliness. The place seemed like no temple at all now that the ark of Yahweh was gone.

The Ark on the Battlefront

When the ark arrived at the battlefront, however, the joy of the soldiers knew no bounds. "They shouted with a great shout, so that the echoes resounded among the hills." Even the

Philistines heard the noise in their camp across the valley. They looked at one another, asking: "What is the meaning of this great shouting in the camp of the Hebrews? Did we not kill thousands among them? Why should they be rejoicing?"

The Philistines sent scouts to find out what was happening among the Hebrews. When the spies returned, they reported that the Hebrews were singing and dancing around a strange box which was set down in the center of their camp. The news terrified the Philistine soldiers. Their fears spread and grew as they talked together. "It must be that their gods have come to help them. Woe to us if their gods are powerful enough to defeat us!"

But the captains of the Philistine army were not so easily frightened. They had no thought of giving up to the Hebrews. They took their soldiers to task for their faint-heartedness. They stood up before them and commanded, "Be strong! Go forward like brave men. You must not surrender to these Hebrews as they did to you in our first battle. Be brave and fight them!"

Soon a second battle began, the Hebrews fighting with new courage because they had the ark. They believed that now Yahweh himself was with them and would make them win. But again they were not strong enough to meet the well-armed and numerous forces of the Philistines. They not only met a worse defeat than before, but they lost the precious ark! And Eli's two sons were killed!

No greater tragedy could be imagined than to have the Philistines capture the sacred chest which the Hebrews had been sure must win the battle for them. How could they ever tell Eli of this terrible loss, and that his own two sons had been killed in the battle! To make matters even worse, some of the Philistines followed up the victory by pursuing the frightened, retreating Hebrews as they fled eastward, chasing them all the way back to the town of Shiloh.

A messenger ran ahead of the fleeing Hebrews to break the sad news of the defeat to Eli. And, as messengers bearing bad tidings always did in ancient times, this man tore his clothes and put dust upon his head as a sign that he brought a message of misfortune. As he entered the village and told the people what had happened, warning them of the approach of the pursuing Philistines, there were cries of grief from all who heard the dreadful news.

Beside the door of his empty shrine sat the old priest, Eli, waiting for the return of the ark. The noise of the wailing people came to his ears and he looked up to see the messenger coming toward him. He knew at once that the worst had happened, yet he was not prepared to hear the panting courier's words as they tumbled from his lips: "Israel has lost the battle! Our men are fleeing before the Philistines and many have been killed! Your two sons, too, are dead! The ark has been captured!" It was too much for the trembling old man. He fell back on his seat, dead.

The Ark Is Held by the Philistines

Very shortly afterwards, the Philistines entered the city and set fire to the houses. Many of the people were killed while others fled screaming into the hills. The Philistines entered the temple itself, broke the sacred vessels, burned everything that would burn, leaving the whole building a smoldering ruin.

Meanwhile, the main part of the Philistine army was marching victoriously home, carrying the ark in triumph back to Ashdod, one of their largest cities. There they placed the Hebrews' treasure in the temple of their God, Dagon.

That night a strange thing happened—for the next morning the image of Dagon was found lying on the floor of the temple. It was put back on its pedestal, but the following morning it was on the floor again, this time its head and hands broken from the body! What could this mean? The Philistines thought it must be that the presence of the ark of Yahweh in their temple had caused this unusual accident to happen.

Shortly after this, there broke out in the city of Ashdod a terrible plague, which caused painful boils to come out on many people's bodies, causing large numbers to die from the disease. At the same time the city was overrun with rats and mice.

Now the Philistines became thoroughly frightened, for they were sure that the ark was responsible for this misfortune. Therefore, they decided to get rid of this fearful object. They sent it to Gath, another Philistine city.

PHILISTINES IN BATTLE

awn by Gertrude Levy, an artist working with John Garstang, from designs of about 1190 B.C.E.
From The Foundations of Bible History: Joshua, Judges, by John Garstang. Used by permission.

Here again, the plague appeared—probably brought by some of the very men who carried the ark from Ashdod to Gath.

In great alarm, the people of Gath sent the ark on to Ekron, a third Philistine city, but the people there had already heard of the plague that had broken out in the neighboring cities, and they cried out: "They are bringing the ark of the God of Israel to us, to kill us and our people." Frantically they called upon the Philistine leaders, begging them to send the ark of Yahweh back to the Hebrews. The leaders, who by this time were just as badly frightened as the people, turned to their own priests and asked: "What must we do with the ark of the God of Israel? Tell us how we may get rid of it."

In those far-off days, priests were supposed to know secret ways of dealing with unknown, evil powers which they believed harmed people. Often these men carried out strange rituals which men supposed would ward off the actions of the unseen, evil spirits. The priests of Ekron began to make the most careful, elaborate plans they could devise and sent their spokesman to the leaders saying: "This is a very serious business, for we are dealing with the God of an enemy people and he is very angry with us. We believe he is a very strong God and his power is in this ark. If you return the ark to the Hebrews, you must not send it back empty, for their God might then become even more angry. You must send an offering to please him. Then perhaps the plague will stop. The offering you send must be five pieces of gold shaped like the boils which have afflicted our people, and five golden mice."

This seems to us a strange kind of offering to make, but the priests believed that these gifts would please the God of the Hebrews and would cause him to stop the plague and take away the rats and mice. They knew, even as early as that, that there was some connection between mice or rats and the disease known today as bubonic plague. They did not, of course, know how to deal with it as doctors do today. They supposed that the invisible evil powers or gods which sent the mice and the disease at the same time would withdraw the evil if a valuable offering were presented to them, made of precious gold in the shape of the very things that accompanied the plague.

The priests continued with their elaborate instructions: "Next you must make a new cart—an old, used one will not do—and hitch it to two milk-cows that have never had yokes on their necks before. Then you must set the ark upon the cart, with a little box beside it containing the five golden boils and the five golden mice. Then you must take their calves away from the cows, and watch closely what the cows will do. If the cows do not follow their calves but start pulling the cart toward the border of the Hebrews' country, then you will know that it was indeed the God of the Hebrews that brought this evil upon us. But if the cows return to their calves, as any mother cow would naturally do, then you will know that the God of the Hebrews had nothing to do with our calamity, but that it was just a coincidence that the disease broke out at the very time that the ark came into our country."

The ancients really believed that detailed and mysterious precautions of this kind were necessary to their safety. So everything was done exactly as the priests had ordered.

The Hebrews Welcome the Ark's Return

Curiously enough, it is said that the cows started off with the cart toward the town of Beth-Shemesh, across the Hebrews' frontier. The Philistines were sure now that Yahweh, the God of the Hebrews, had caused the plague. They were relieved to feel that they were rid of the ark. They hoped that their golden offerings would so please the God of the Hebrews that he would remove the plague from them!

As the cart bearing the ark approached Beth-Shemesh, some Hebrew farmers, reaping wheat in a field, heard the cows lowing. The men looked up to see their precious ark coming down the road. At once they threw down their scythes and ran, shouting with joy, to meet the procession. The few Philistines who had followed at a distance, to watch the ark's journey, quickly turned and went back to their own country.

So thankful were the Hebrews to see their ark again that they took the cows and immediately offered them as a sacrifice to Yahweh, using a great rock beside the road as an altar and breaking up the wood of the cart for a fire.

But rejoicing soon turned to sorrow for the people of Beth-Shemesh. Not many days after, some of the men who had opened the ark to look into it were taken ill. Could it be that the deadly germs had infected the box and now were causing the same terrible disease that had raged in the Philistine cities? In any case, the disease spread among the Hebrews until about seventy people died. This alarmed and puzzled the people of Beth-Shemesh. Why should this happen? Their own precious ark— the ark which meant to them the presence of Yahweh—should not bring calamity to Yahweh's own people. They could understand why the Philistines should suffer at the hands of Yahweh, but now the ark was at home again and all should be well. Yahweh must still be angry for some reason. Perhaps he wanted the sacred box put in a temple, such as the one at Shiloh. But Shiloh was now in ruins. Was there another shrine somewhere that might be a fitting place for the ark?

Then someone remembered a shrine in Kirjath-Jearim, not far away. They sent word to the men of that village and they came and took the ark back with them. There in the shrine at Kirjath-Jearim it remained for many years, apparently without any harm coming to the people.

The Hebrews Now Know They Must Unite

These tragic experiences which the Hebrews had been suffering, while the Philistines were continuing to advance farther into the hills, made the Hebrew farmers wonder what was to become of them. Why had Yahweh permitted them to be defeated—twice over—even when they had carried the ark with them into the battle? Had Yahweh forsaken them, or was he just not a strong enough war-god to give his people victory? Could it be, perhaps, that the fault was not Yahweh's but their own? Up to this time the Hebrews had never been able to gather all of their tribes together at one time to meet the enemy, but only a few here and a few there. This was not enough to face so powerful a foe as the Philistines, and so well-armed a force as they could bring to battle.

Why should not all of the tribes unite now against the mighty invaders from the coast? Surely, if they could only find a leader whom all the tribes would be willing to follow, they might muster a force strong enough to be victorious and thus save their homes, and remain in the land of Canaan. There were men among the Hebrews who were asking these questions and making up their minds to look for a leader who would be able to bring all the tribes together under his leadership. They hoped that it was not already too late to bring about such an end to their troubles.

The Philistines already held most of the plains and had made their way into the hills at many points. It was becoming more and more certain that nothing but a united front against the Philistines would do. There must be union of all the tribes—they must form one people, standing together, and facing together the common danger which threatened them all!

"A king! That is what we must have!" said some. "Other peoples around us have kings. We must have a king—and a kingdom. We must be one nation, and not a collection of jealous tribes, often quarreling and fighting with one another."

"But that is not the way of our fathers," said others. "We have always had elders in each of our tribes. And we have had great chieftains who led, now this tribe and now that one, or several of them, when danger threatened—and they have had success against our desert enemies. But always we have had freedom within our own tribes."

"But," said those who proposed having a king, "the Philistines are mightier than any enemy we have ever met before. It would be better to have a king of our own than to fall under the power of a Philistine king."

Even though more and more Hebrews began to see the necessity of having one ruler, a very serious question still needed an answer.

"Suppose we do decide that only a king can save us—who shall the king be? From which of the tribes shall he be chosen? You see—it is no easy solution of our troubles to say 'We must have a king!'"

Thus this idea of having a king to rule over all the Hebrew tribes was talked about everywhere, among all the Hebrew tribes. Some of the older men were giving much of their time in the effort to find a man who might be chosen to rule. It was not the way of their fathers, they knew. There were many among the tribes who refused to believe it was the right thing to do, for it would mean that each of the tribes would have to give up some of its independence, and would have to obey the orders of a great chief who would have greater power than any of the tribal leaders had. Yet to have a king over all seemed to be the only way that offered any hope, if the Philistine advance was to be stopped.

8

A King to Unite the Tribes

An Old Man Watches and Prays

In a village called Ramah, nestled in the hills near the southern border of the territory of Ephraim, lived an old man who was greatly respected by all the people of his district. This man Samuel was priest at the shrine that stood on top of the hill above the village. The people of the village and of the surrounding country not only came to this shrine to make sacrifices and to celebrate special festivals, but also came personally to the priest Samuel, to ask him to inquire of Yahweh in their behalf. They asked for help about matters which they could not of themselves decide. For example, someone might come to Samuel to ask whether or not he should take the journey he had contemplated. Another might ask if he should leave home and join those who were fighting the Philistines. Or still another might ask where his lost sheep had strayed and how they might be found. Because Samuel seemed so able to answer their questions, they called him "the Seer of Ramah." It seemed to them that this old man had a kind of "second sight"—a God-given power—to see things that others could not see.

Now Samuel was one of those who kept watching and hoping that a leader might soon be found who would be able to save the defeated and discouraged Hebrew tribesmen from the advancing Philistines. Over and over he had prayed to Yahweh asking for some sign by which they might know who was fitted to do this great task. Samuel was hoping that he himself might find Israel's future king.

While he performed his duties as seer and priest, he used to watch closely the many people who came to him for advice and help. He must have often thought to himself: "I wonder if today the man will come who will be the king we are seeking?" Samuel was sure that the man they so much needed must appear soon,

69

before it became too late to save his people. Samuel knew, of course, that it was not going to be easy for any one man to be accepted as king over all the tribes. He knew, too, that it was not the way of the fathers before them, to set up kings to rule over them.

But for years the Hebrews had been steadily losing to these Philistines one village after another in the highlands of Ephraim. Enemy garrisons were now stationed in village after village, and the Hebrews who had survived the battles were virtually slaves of the Philistine conquerors. More and more families had been moving farther east and making new homes for themselves where the Philistines had not yet advanced. Never before had there been so serious a situation for the Hebrews as now. The tribes must stand together or fall together.

The more Samuel thought over this problem, the more firmly he became convinced that Yahweh would somehow point out the man who was to be their king, one who could lead the tribes to victory, and who could make one nation of them at last.

An Old Legend About Samuel

We do not know how many people of the other Hebrew tribes knew Samuel or respected him as the villagers of Ramah did, but in one of the two books in the Bible called by Samuel's name there is a story that describes the part he took in finding the first king of Israel. This is how the story is told.[1]

There was a man of the Benjamin tribe named Kish, who lived near the town of Gibeah. Kish was a wealthy farmer and owned great pasture lands on which he raised large numbers of animals. One day some donkeys strayed away from his fields and became lost, so Kish called his tall and handsome son Saul, and said: "Take one of the servants and hunt for the lost animals."

So Saul and a servant started out over the hills to search for the donkeys. After many days of wandering, without finding any trace of the missing donkeys, Saul became discouraged and was ready to give up the search. "Let us go home," he said to the servant. "By this time my father will be more anxious about us than about the lost donkeys, for we have been gone a long time."

---

[1] I Samuel, chapter 9.

On their way back home, Saul and his servant arrived in the neighborhood of Ramah, where Samuel, the "Seer," lived; but Saul had never heard of the old man. His servant, however, had been talking with some of the people they had met along the road. The servant, therefore, said to Saul: "I have been told that a Seer named Samuel lives here. The people call him a 'man of God,' for he is also a priest. Let us go to him, for perhaps he can tell us where to go to find the lost donkeys."

But Saul, realizing that they had exhausted all their food and supplies on the long journey, replied: "How can we go to this Seer? For we have nothing to give him. What can we pay him for his advice?"

"I have a small piece of silver with me," said the servant.

AN ASIATIC NOMAD

In this picture of about 1900 B.C.E., found in an Egyptian tomb at Benihasan, a nomad walks beside his donkey and plays his lyre. He has a waterskin slung from his back. On his saddle cloth are tied a throw-stick and a spear.

"Perhaps the Seer will accept it and be kind to us, and tell us what to do."

"Well said," replied Saul. "Come, let us go to find Samuel's house."

As they walked toward the village of Ramah, they met some young women, carrying large earthenware jugs on their shoulders, who were going to draw water from a near-by well. "Is the Seer here?" Saul asked one of the women. "Yes," was the reply, "you will see him if you wait by the city gate. He will soon be passing there on his way to make a sacrifice on the hilltop outside the city, for today is a feast day."

Saul and the servant, therefore, did as they were told. They had not waited long outside the gate when a man came out, whom they asked: "Will you kindly tell us where the Seer's house is?" "I am the Seer," replied the man, who was indeed Samuel himself.

Then Saul told Samuel of their long search for the lost donkeys. Could he possibly tell them where the animals were? Samuel answered, "I cannot stop now. I am on my way to the high place where we shall celebrate a festival. But come with me. We can talk later."

Gladly Saul accepted the old man's invitation, and walked with him up to the hilltop. There a number of villagers were already gathered. An animal was being roasted on the altar. Samuel gave Saul and his servant places of honor during the meal that followed and afterwards took them back to his home in the village to spend the night.

The two men sat and talked until late in the night. The longer Samuel talked with Saul, the more convinced he became that here beside him was the man he had been hoping to find. So persistent—so ready to learn—so strong in body—so tall and handsome! Samuel had never before seen such a man among all his tribesmen.

In the morning, as Saul was preparing to leave, the old priest asked that they might have a few words together alone. So the servant was told to go on ahead, while Samuel and Saul walked along more leisurely.

When the two were by themselves, Samuel said: "Do not be anxious about the lost donkeys, for they have been found."

Then, to Saul's great surprise, the Seer went on: "But I have found you too, for you are the man I have been looking for. You are the one who should lead our people in their struggle against the Philistines. I believe Yahweh has told me that you are the man."

Saul, too astonished to speak, could only stare wonderingly at the Seer. When his amazement had passed, he said: "But how can I be the one to do this great and difficult work! I come from the smallest of all the tribes, the tribe of Benjamin. And my family is one of the least important in our tribe. How can you say this to me?"

The Seer would not listen to Saul's objection. "You are the very man to lead all the tribes," he said. "I am sure that the people will accept you. Some day they will ask you to be their king. It is best that our king should come from the smallest tribe, for the men of the greater tribes will be less jealous of your little tribe of Benjamin than of any other. Do not be afraid because of the greatness of your office as king. Yahweh, our God, will be with you. It is his people whom you will be leading."

Samuel then took a small bottle of sweet-smelling oil from his belt. He poured the oil into Saul's hair, and kissed him and said, "This is a sign that Saul, the son of Kish, has been set apart by Yahweh to be king of Israel." This brief ceremony was performed while the two were alone. For the present it was a secret between Samuel and Saul.

Saul Finds New Associates

The two walked on together and the conversation continued. "As you go home," said Samuel, "you will pass the camp of the patriots, on a hill near the garrison of the Philistines outside your own village of Gibeah. You will hear their pipes and drums and harps playing wild music, and you will hear them shouting and singing wild songs. Perhaps you have always regarded these fellows as coarse and barbaric. You have been too proud to associate yourself with them. But I tell you, Saul, you need to get acquainted with these men now. These young enthusiasts are afraid of nothing. They believe they are acting and speaking for Yahweh, our God. Among them are some young men who do not call themselves prophets but 'sons of the prophets.' Some people sneer at them; but you should not do so, Saul, for these men are your best allies. Go into their camp and spend a night there. Join with them in their songs and dances, for you too must be filled with the same patriotic passion they have if you are to take your place as champion of Israel against the Philistines."

Just as Samuel had said, Saul found the camp of the patriots near Gibeah, only a little way off from the Philistine garrison. He stopped with them to watch and listen. Soon he was carried away by their exciting dancing and shouting. He too danced and leaped about, singing and shouting with them:

Rise! Fight for Yahweh our God!
Drive out the enemy who would destroy us!
In the name of Yahweh, O men of Israel, strike a blow for freedom!
Save our people and our land from the Philistines!

Under the spell of this experience, Saul returned home. He told his family and friends of how Samuel had helped him find the lost donkeys, but he said nothing of the secret between himself and the Seer, or of his experience with the "sons of the prophets." He returned quietly to the daily round of duties on his father's farm.

A New Threat Appears[2]

Within a month after Saul's return home, the people of Jabesh-Gilead, many miles to the east across the Jordan, got into trouble. For some time now, the Hebrews who had settled on the eastern side of the Jordan had lived undisturbed by the advancing Philistines. Their enemies were the Ammonites from the deserts still farther south, who were seeking more fertile lands. But for many years the people of Jabesh-Gilead had not been molested by anyone, and they had almost forgotten to give any thought to what they would do if attacked.

Then suddenly an army of Ammonites from the east appeared outside the city gates and demanded their surrender. The people of Jabesh-Gilead were stunned. They knew they were helpless. In desperation they sent word to the Ammonite commander, saying: "We will surrender provided you make reasonable terms with us."

---
[2] I Samuel 11: 1-15.

But the Ammonite commander answered haughtily: "I will make terms with you on one condition that all your right eyes be put out."

The rulers of Jabesh-Gilead were speechless with terror. How could they consent to such a fate? If the right eye of every soldier were put out, they would be as blind men—for it was the practice of foot soldiers to hold their shields in the left hand and so protect the left eye, while the right eye was used to see the enemy.

But what could the men of the city do? If only they could be given a little time, they might get some reinforcements from the tribes across the Jordan. They had small reason to hope for any assistance, for what had Jabesh-Gilead ever done to help the Hebrews across the river? But a small hope was better than

A CANAANITE ARK

The Israelite ark at Shiloh may have been a chest similar in shape to this restoration of a Megiddo shrine.

no hope at all. So they begged the Ammonite commander: "Give us a week's time to make up our minds."

The Ammonite commander was so sure that nobody could come to help this far-away city of Jabesh-Gilead that he haughtily decided to grant this small request. It would do no harm.

Greatly relieved, the rulers of Jabesh-Gilead sent messengers as quickly as possible across the Jordan to different Hebrew settlements and towns. Everywhere they went, they told of the terrible Ammonite threat to their city and begged for help.

In due time some of these messengers reached the town of Gibeah where Saul lived. A large crowd gathered in the market place. Shocked by the terrible news the messengers brought, the people lifted up their voices and wept.

It was in the late afternoon. Saul was just coming back from the field behind a pair of oxen. "What is the trouble with the people?" he asked. "Why are they weeping?"

Saul heard then of the awful fate that awaited the people of Jabesh-Gilead, and his anger was stirred. He felt power rushing into him—a very great power. He thought it was power from Yahweh. Saul remembered his talk with Samuel and Samuel's command to him.

"This is my time!" he thought to himself. "Someone must take the lead. I shall gather an army and we shall save our brothers from these arrogant Ammonites."

At once Saul sprang into action. Then and there he called for volunteers. Then and there he picked up his ax and slew his two oxen with which he had been ploughing. He cut their bodies into pieces. He appointed messengers. He gave to each one a piece of ox flesh, and he sent them forth to the Hebrew settlements and towns all over the countryside.

All that night the messengers ran through the land, carrying the grim and bloody pieces of ox flesh and giving the alarm. "Come, all you men of Israel! Follow Saul across the Jordan against the Ammonites! See this piece of ox flesh I hold in my hands. Saul killed his own two oxen and gave each of us a piece of their flesh to show you. By this bloody sign you know how serious matters are. Saul says, 'If you do not come to the battle now, there will soon be nothing left of your own oxen but pieces like these we carry!'"

These frantic appeals were irresistible. With great speed, men from many settlements rushed to follow Saul. Before the Ammonites knew what was happening, Saul's forces had surrounded the Ammonite army outside Jabesh-Gilead. Early one morning they made a surprise attack, and fought until midday when the sun was hot. Those of the Ammonites who were not killed fled in confusion back to their own country.

A King at Last!

As the men of Saul's army returned to their homes after the battle, they carried the report of this amazing victory, and of Saul's able leadership in the emergency, to all parts of the country. In village after village, through all the tribes, we might have heard men saying joyfully: "At last a great leader has appeared! Here is the man we need. He can act quickly and courageously. He has been able to gather men from all the tribes to fight side by side and to win a great battle. We must make him our king, to lead us against the Philistines!"

In their enthusiasm for Saul, the people forgot their tribal jealousies. Even the men of the larger tribes seemed proud that the small and unimportant tribe of Benjamin could produce so excellent a leader. All seemed to agree that Saul was their man.

Someone (the Bible story says it was Samuel) sent word to the people of all tribes. "Come to Gilgal down by the Jordan river. There let us sing to Yahweh our songs of thanksgiving and let us make sacrifices and pray that Yahweh may bring us peace, and before the altar let us crown Saul as king of us all."

Everywhere the response to this call was enthusiastic. Thousands of men and women, soldiers and other leaders of tribes far and near, traveled to Gilgal. There the old priest Samuel, in the presence of the crowds, once more poured sweet oil on Saul's hair and kissed him. And before all the multitudes he proclaimed in a loud voice: "In the name of Yahweh our God I appoint this day Saul, the son of Kish, king of Israel!"

Then all the crowd shouted with a great shout: "Long live our king!" And the priests took oxen and sheep and slew them on the stone altars that were in this place. And all the people feasted and danced and made glad their hearts.

9

A Warrior King with a Warrior Son

The Warrior Son

Among the soldiers in the crowd that gathered to crown Saul king of Israel was his son, Jonathan. Perhaps Jonathan had seen his father on that dreadful day when he killed his own pair of oxen. And now on this great day in Gilgal when Jonathan heard the crowds cheering his father's name, he resolved with all his heart to stand by his father whatever happened, so that together they might save their people from the Philistines.

The Warrior Father

As for Saul himself, he accepted seriously the responsibility of his new position. There was no time to lose, for even while Saul and his army had been occupied with the exploit to save Jabesh-Gilead, the Philistines had been advancing their positions. In one town after another in the hills the Philistines had placed fresh garrisons, and were holding the Hebrews captive in their own towns.

Saul returned to his old home in Gibeah and immediately called for men. From those who came, he picked out three thousand who had already proven their valor in the battle of Jabesh-Gilead. He then divided this force into three equal divisions. One he placed under the command of Jonathan and kept in the town of Gibeah. Saul himself commanded the other two divisions for the time being. He stationed one of these divisions in Bethel and the other in Michmash. These two towns held positions of advantage, since they were both on high land, one on one side of a deep valley and the other on the opposite side.

Thus Saul had two important observation posts from which he could watch the Philistine garrisons. If the Philistines should make any move to attack him, Saul would now be ready to call his forces together quickly; or, if he saw a favorable time to open an attack on the enemy, he was in a position to do so.

Jonathan Opens the Revolt[1]

The way hostilities actually began, however, was not according to Saul's plan. It was due rather to a rash act of his son Jonathan at Gibeah, where he had been waiting idly with his part of the Hebrew forces. Perhaps Jonathan grew tired of doing nothing. In any case, he went out one night with only a few of his men to the very edge of the Philistine camp near Gibeah. There stood a stone pillar or stele, which the Philistines had erected to commemorate their victory over the Hebrews. Jonathan and his men knocked down and broke the stone pillar, and left it lying flat on the ground.

In the morning, when the Philistines discovered the ruined pillar, they were so angry that they immediately sent out an alarm up and down the valley. "The Hebrews have revolted! Arise! Fight!"

When word of the tragedy reached the Philistines in Michmash across the valley, they became so excited that a large part of their garrison left the fort there, and started out to raid the countryside.

In the meantime, Saul had returned to Gibeah. And nearly half of his soldiers near Michmash had for some reason gone away on another expedition across the Jordan, perhaps to repel a new attack on the Ammonites. This left the camp near Michmash with only about six hundred men.

On came those angered Philistine raiders back toward Michmash. They were sure that they could quickly crush the Hebrew garrison there and so make a speedy end of this revolt. On learning of their approach, the frightened Hebrew inhabitants of Michmash were panic-stricken. They were sure that the enemy would easily overcome the small Hebrew army. So they fled out of the town and hid themselves in caves and thickets in the

---

[1] The stories in this chapter are based on I Samuel 13; and 14: 1-46. At a number of points this ancient record is confused and inconsistent. In I Samuel 13:3 the translation in the King James version is misleading. In this rewriting, the author has sought to create a consistent story.

hills around the town, and behind rocks, and even in old empty cisterns.

Another Daring Adventure

While all this was going on, Jonathan, waiting idly in Gibeah, distinguished himself once more. Early one morning, accompanied by his armor-bearer, he slipped away secretly from the camp in Gibeah, without his father's knowledge. His plan was to attack the reduced Philistine garrison in Michmash while the raiding parties were absent. Jonathan and his armor-bearer made their way to the base of a steep cliff, between Michmash and Gibeah, and began to climb up. They knew that at the top of this cliff was a Philistine fort which they wished to enter by surprise. But before they reached the top, the Philistines in the fort caught sight of them. Instead of rushing out to push the two Hebrews off the cliff or to capture them, the Philistine soldiers mockingly cheered the boldness of these two lone Hebrews, and dared them to come all the way up to the fort. "Come up to us," they shouted, "and we will show you a thing (or two)."[2]

To the astonishment of the gaping soldiers in the fort, the two adventurers accepted the challenge and clambered up the rocks. Once at the top, Jonathan and his armor-bearer leaped into the fort, and began to strike about them with their swords, cutting down every Philistine who approached. The suddenness of this unexpected action caused those in front to fall back against the soldiers behind them. Soon all the Philistines in the fort were frantically trying to get out of reach of the flailing swords of the two Hebrews, and rushed out of the fort in a panic.

Just at this moment, one of the Philistine raiding parties returned. Ignorant of what was happening, they were met by the terror-stricken soldiers from the fort—whereupon they too became frightened and beat a disorderly retreat. The whole Philistine garrison was in complete confusion.

Meanwhile, Saul was unaware of Jonathan's absence, but he could hear the uproar, and looking across the valley he could see people running out of the town. "What has happened?" he wondered. Quickly he ordered a count to be taken of his men,

---

[2] I Samuel 14:12.

THE GORGE OF MICHMASH

This is the crag climbed by Jonathan and his armor-bearer.

to learn who was absent. To his surprise he found that it was Jonathan and his armor-bearer. It did not seem possible that Jonathan and his armor-bearer alone could have caused all this disorder in the Philistine fort. What should Saul do in this emergency?

Saul was worried, and called the priest to bring the *ephod*[3] and to ask it what Yahweh wanted done. But even as the priest was in the act of drawing out of the *ephod* the stone that he thought would have the answer of God on it, the tumult in the Philistine camp became wilder and louder. Saul rushed away and gave orders to his soldiers to march forth at once to attack Michmash without waiting for the priest's answer from the *ephod*.

Now it was no easy walk from Gibeah across the valley to Michmash, and Saul realized that speed was all-important. He therefore commanded that no one should stop to eat along the way. Indeed, no one should eat anything until he returned to Gibeah in the evening. "Cursed be the man that eateth any food until evening," he said. "Only one thing is important. We must have our vengeance on our enemies today."

The march across the valley was made in record time. The arrival of more Hebrew soldiers added to the panic of the Philistines. Saul's men joined Jonathan and his armor-bearer, and soon they were in full pursuit of the fleeing enemy forces. Even the inhabitants of Michmash, who had earlier hidden themselves in caves, came swarming out to join their fellows in chasing the Philistines in their mad retreat, until they were lost in a deep woods.

In Their Hunger They Forgot

By the time the Hebrew soldiers were back in Michmash, they were hungry and faint. In fact, they were so famished they forgot Saul's command not to eat until they returned to Gibeah at nightfall. Without ceremony, they fell upon the spoil they found left in the Philistine camp. They took sheep and oxen and calves, and slew them, and ate the flesh raw, without even taking time to let the blood drain out on the ground as a gift to Yahweh. They were too faint to obey the ancient law that said that the

---

[3] See Chapter 5 in this book.

blood must be drained out on the ground as a gift, for the blood is the life and belongs to God, the Giver of all life.

It was near nightfall when the victorious army returned to Gibeah, where their king waited anxiously to learn how they had fared. Saul listened with pride to the story of the bravery of his son Jonathan and of his armor-bearer. "Yahweh be praised!" he said. "He hath put our enemies to flight."

But when he heard the story of how the hungry men had eaten, in spite of his command and curse, Saul was shocked and angry. He was also afraid because they had disobeyed, not only their king but also the ancient law of Moses. Yahweh would be angry because, before eating, they had not given back to him the blood, the life that belonged to him. But Saul could not be too harsh with his men. After all they had fought hard and had risked their lives. They were famished and faint when they disobeyed. Perhaps Yahweh would even yet forgive.

So Saul hurried out where stood an altar for sacrifice. His priests slew some sheep and oxen. The blood was properly drained out upon the ground as a gift to Yahweh, their God. A prayer of thanksgiving was sung. The flesh was roasted and parts were burned completely as a gift to Yahweh. And then, and not until then, the soldiers were permitted to eat the rest.

When the Ephod Gave No Answer

Saul, however, was not content with what had been accomplished. He wondered if he should not go down again against the Philistines sometime at night, and take more spoils. He felt that not one single man among them should be left alive. When Saul asked his men for their advice, they answered: "Do whatever seemeth good to thee." But Saul was not satisfied. He must again ask the *ephod*.

So he went with his priest into the shrine where he felt near to Yahweh, his God, and stood before the *ephod*.

"Shall I go down again after the Philistines?" he asked. "Wilt thou deliver them into the hand of Israel?"

But try as he would, the priest could obtain no answer from the *ephod*. Perhaps there came out from the *ephod* neither the white stone which would mean "Yes," nor the black stone which meant "No," but only a gray stone or a curiously marked one which meant "No answer." When this happened, it was believed that for some reason Yahweh was angry and therefore withheld his answer. What could be the reason for Yahweh's silence? Could it be that someone else had disobeyed the order forbidding the eating of food that day?

Finally in the morning, Saul called the chiefs together and said: "Do any of you know who it is who has done wrong? As Yahweh liveth who saved Israel, we must find out. Even though it be Jonathan, my son, he shall surely die."

But there was not a man among all the people that answered Saul. Finally Saul said: "We shall cast lots. Let all of you be on one side and Jonathan and I on the other side."

Then Saul took up the lots and prayed. "Yahweh, show us the right one." When the lots were thrown, Jonathan and Saul were taken and the people escaped.

Then Saul cast lots between himself and Jonathan. And Jonathan was taken.

"Tell me, my son, what hast thou done?"

Then Jonathan told his father. "While we were returning from chasing the Philistines in the woods, we came upon some bushes on which hung a few honey combs. I dipped my fingers into the comb and ate a little of the honey. It was not until I had eaten that I heard of your command. Must I die for such a thing as this?"

Saul was afraid to break his oath even to save his son. He feared that Yahweh might do something even worse to punish him and his people if he did not stand by his oath.

"Thou shalt surely die, Jonathan." The voice sounded harsh and cold—the voice of a king, not the voice of a father.

This was too much for the soldiers who stood by. Jonathan must not be killed. He was too valuable a man to lose in this way. Had he not twice led attacks which had brought defeat to the enemy? His life must somehow be saved. Might not a valuable animal be substituted as a sacrifice, in place of the king's son, to please Yahweh? "So the men rescued Jonathan, that he died not."

Saul was in deadly earnest in his purpose to please his God, and he followed the ways of doing this which were commonly believed in his day. To us these ways seem cruel and unreason-able, but three thousand years ago, when Saul lived, they were commonly accepted ways of thinking.

During the rest of his life as king of Israel, Saul had to fight many battles against the Philistines. He was, indeed, a warrior-king, and kept the fighting forces of his people strong and ready to resist at any point the continuing attacks of the Philistines. This is really his claim to fame—that he succeeded in welding the scattered, jealous tribes of the Hebrews into the beginnings of a nation. Had it not been for his leadership at this time, the Philistines might have succeeded in taking over the whole land of Canaan. They might have prevented the Hebrews from ever building their kingdom.

10

A Strong Man Weakens

UNDER KING SAUL THE TIDE of victory in Canaan began to turn against the Philistines in favor of the Hebrews. The first king of Israel was proving to be just the kind of leader that was needed to draw the tribes together in defense of their people against their common enemy. Messengers ran along the roads and into the villages shouting the news of each triumph. Neighbors in the hilltop towns talked excitedly as they gathered to share the good news, and to sing the praises of their successful king.

Yet for all his many and sometimes brilliant victories over the Philistines, Saul was never able to conquer them completely or to drive them entirely out of the land. This fact troubled the king greatly, for there was nothing he wanted more than to free his people, once and for all, from the threat of these rival invaders.[1]

A Confused and Divided Personality

As Saul thought to himself about his failure to win complete victory over the Philistines, he became more unhappy and fretful in his mind. Indeed he became so greatly changed that all who saw him, especially his closest friends, began to talk to one another anxiously about their king.

"Have you noticed," one would whisper to his companion, "how suddenly Saul flies into a rage over the most trifling things?"

"Yes, and several times I have seen him seized with a fit of gloom and despair so that he looks almost like a madman."

"He seldom smiles any more, and those of us who are nearest to him hardly know how to please him."

"He is still a great leader in battle, with a courage and skill beyond that of any other man I know, but I'm afraid of what he may do when these attacks come upon him."

---

[1] The story in this chapter is based on I Samuel 16:14-23, and on the 23rd Psalm.

Perhaps it was not only Saul's inability to win a final and sweeping victory over the Philistines that preyed upon his mind. There is a story told that Samuel, who had been first to recognize Saul's qualities of leadership, had begun to lose confidence in him. It must have been a terrible blow to Saul to feel that the Seer of Ramah no longer believed in him—the man who had encouraged Saul to take command of Israel's forces, and who had anointed him king of Israel before anyone else knew of the plan. There was even a rumor that Samuel was already seeking another man to take Saul's place as king.

When danger arose, Saul could still take command of the army and win battles against the enemy. But during the times between battles, when there was no call for quick action, the king lost that steadiness and vigor which made him a great leader. At such times he would often sit for hours by himself, refusing to see anyone, and he would brood gloomily alone. His clouded, haunted mind would imagine all sorts of evil things about his best friends. His mood would change so suddenly that within a few moments he would hate and fear those whom he had always loved and trusted. He became suspicious of men who had always been his most loyal supporters. He looked upon his chief leaders in the kingdom as rivals to his throne, and his jealousy of them grew fierce and threatening. Saul's friends almost welcomed the times when some new enemy attack would come, for this would bring the king quickly out of his gloom and set him at the head of his army as the brave, alert leader of earlier days.

The slow weakening of his mind and spirit finally proved to be Saul's undoing, but it was sad and alarming for his friends to watch him lose ground. They did not know, of course, what was causing this strange and tragic change in their king. It seemed to them that, if Yahweh had really chosen Saul as the leader to save his people from the Philistines, as even the Seer of Ramah had said in the beginning, Yahweh had now for some reason given him up.

"What has happened," they would ask, "to the spirit of Yahweh that came to Saul when he joined the group of singing, dancing prophets after Samuel appointed him? Surely, an evil spirit has taken possession of him to cause this dreadful illness."[2] In

2 I Samuel 16:14.

those days, it was believed that all illness, whether of the body or of the mind, was caused by evil spirits which entered a man and changed him.

A Shepherd Is Summoned

Saul himself, during the times when the attacks of gloom and melancholy were not upon him, was aware of the change that had taken place in him. He was just as eager as anyone else to discover a remedy for his illness.

There were ways in which such sicknesses were treated three thousand years ago, and doubtless the court physicians tried all the remedies they knew, but nothing they could do seemed to bring a cure.

Finally someone suggested that they try to find the best musician in the land, bring him to the court, and have him play and sing for the king whenever one of his fits of despair came upon him. 'If sweet music is played, the king's mind will be taken away from his troubles and anxieties," said the man who advised this experiment. Saul thought well of this suggestion, so that he himself gave the order to his servants: "Go out and search the kingdom for a man who is a skillful musician, and bring him to me."

One of the young men then spoke up: "I have heard of a lad, living in Bethlehem, who is said to be a very wonderful player of the harp. It is David, one of the sons of Jesse, a farmer of Bethlehem. This David has been herding sheep ever since he was a small boy, and through the long hours he has spent alone with his sheep on the hillsides, he has played a great deal on his flute and his harp. The neighbors all say that no one else can play as beautifully as he. And they say also that David sings beautifully. He has even composed some songs of his own that are known by the people all over the south country. They love David's songs."

At once Saul sent a messenger to Bethlehem.

When he arrived at the door of Jesse's home, he announced that he had come with a summons from King Saul. "The King wishes your son David to come at once to Gibeah to be his court musician."

The father was taken by surprise, but pleased to have his son

thus honored. Jesse ordered a slave to run to the field and bring
David at once.

Soon "a ruddy youth, fair-eyed and good to look at" appeared
before the messenger. Some say he was light-haired, with bright
blue eyes and light skin, quite different from most of the Hebrew
people, who were dark-skinned and black-haired.

The king's messenger was charmed by the young man's looks
and manner. The two sat down together in the garden. As they
chatted, the messenger drew from David some stories of his life.
Forced to pass many hours of each day alone on the hillsides
watching sheep, David had spent much time playing his pipe and
his harp. He loved his music. He also liked to sing as he played
his harp. Why shouldn't he make up his own songs? Of course,
he sang the old ballads, but sometimes he felt like singing a new

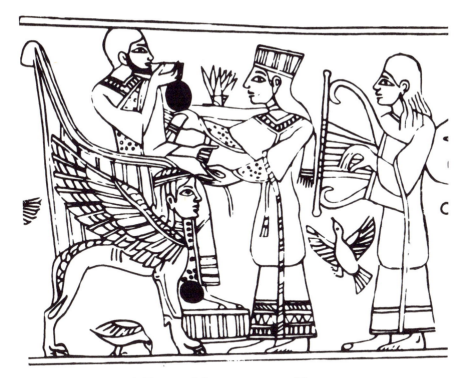

A KING OF MEGIDDO AND HIS MUSICIAN
*In this painting found on a wall at Benihasan, the king takes a drink and
listens to a lyre player.*

song. Yes, he had taught some of his songs to the neighbors. And they loved to sing them together.

"But herding sheep is not always so pleasant, is it?" asked the messenger from the king. Then David began with stories of his adventures with lions and bears that sometimes came out of the woods to take lambs from his flock. He had much practice in the art of stone throwing with a sling. He had often been able to aim accurately enough to hit a running wolf, and he had once fought a lion singlehanded.

These adventures were a natural part of a shepherd's life. David was quite sure of himself when herding sheep. But to be asked to go to the king's court and play for the king! This was exciting to think about, but it made David feel timid and anxious. Could he play well enough for a king?

While the two men were talking together, Jesse, the father, was preparing to obey the king's summons. He brought an ass from its stall and loaded it with a supply of bread and cheese, bottles of wine, and goat's meat as a present for the king. Before nightfall his shepherd son was on his way to the royal court.

His Music Heals

It was not until David stepped through the doorway of the king's chamber, and was left alone with the king, that he realized the danger he was in. For at the very time of his coming, Saul was suffering from one of his dreaded attacks. There before him David saw a large man, sitting alone, his staring eyes looking straight ahead into space. Mumbling sounds were coming from his close-pressed lips. The king seemed not to notice David's entrance into the room, did not once look up at him, but remained sitting, half-sprawling in his chair as though completely worn out, his mouth twitching, and his hands clasping and unclasping nervously.

"What shall I do?" thought David. "Will he notice me if I begin playing? Will the music soothe him, or will it make him angry so that he will drive me away?" Quietly David held his harp and began to play softly some of the tunes he had learned so well out there on the hills of Bethlehem. At first King Saul seemed not to hear the music, but remained motionless, gazing straight ahead as if he were straining his eyes to see something just out of sight at the end of the long room. The king's mind seemed to be wandering in dark places, and his face was pale and drawn.

As David plucked the strings of his harp, he never took his eyes from the king, but watched him intently to watch any effect which his playing might bring. As the minutes went by, David soon lost himself in the spell of his own sweet music that came from his beloved harp. Never had he played so enchantingly, and never did so much depend upon the effect of his artistry.

Softly, then, he began to sing some of the old songs of the past which every Hebrew loved, songs about the heroes of their people's history—of Abraham who first came to this land from Ur, long, long ago. He sang of Isaac and of Jacob, and of their wanderings over the hills and plains of ancient Canaan, before the Egyptians had come to possess it. He sang of the oppression of the Hebrews in Egypt and of the glorious deliverance which Moses had wrought. So absorbed was David in the songs he sang, that he did not know how long he sat there. Then he remembered what had brought him, and he looked up without interrupting the flow of his music.

David thought he saw a flicker of interest in Saul's eyes, as the king turned his head toward him for a moment. David continued to sing to the accompaniment of his harp, turning now to some of the songs he himself had composed—songs about Saul and his victories over the Philistines, of the new hopes which Saul's leadership had kindled in the hearts of his people. Now David knew that Saul was listening, for he saw a smile cross the face of the king. Slowly Saul sat upright in his chair and gazed toward the player, a pleased expression on his face. No longer was the haunted look in Saul's eyes, but a look of interest, of close attention to these new songs he had never heard before about his own great service to his people, and the bright future to which they now looked forward. The "sweet singer of Israel" had brought peace to the fevered brain of the sick king. David's deep-toned harp and melodious voice had worked their curing magic, and had driven away the dark shadows from Saul's mind. One more song David sang, a psalm which he had composed out on the lonely hillsides of Bethlehem.

The Lord is my shepherd, I shall not want . . .
Yea, though I walk through the valley of the shadow of death
I will fear no evil—for Thou art with me;
Thy rod and thy staff, they comfort me . . .
Surely goodness and mercy shall follow me all the days of my life,
And I will dwell in the presence of the Lord forever.

The music and the thought in the beautiful psalm reached the heart of the king. When it ended, he rose from his chair and came toward David. He placed his hand quietly on the young man's head and spoke softly to him: "You must stay with me, my son," he said. "I shall send a message to your father to ask him to let you remain here, for I need you. Your harp and your sweet songs have refreshed me. I have never heard such wonderful music before."

David was pleased and proud that the great man spoke thus to him, for now David knew that the king loved him and would trust him. David was hardly prepared, however, to hear Saul's next words: "You shall be my armor-bearer and go with me whenever I must lead our army to battle." This would mean that a place would be made in the king's house for David, and he would be one of Saul's nearest and most constant attendants, almost like a member of the royal family.

11

The Giant and the Shepherd Youth

THE PHILISTINE ARMY WAS DRAWN UP in battle array on a hillside somewhere near the southwestern border of Saul's kingdom.
Saul's army had taken a position on a hillside on the opposite
slope of the same valley above which the Philistines were encamped. King Saul was at the head of Israel's army, and with
him was David, his young armor-bearer. The two forces faced
each other menacingly.[1]

The Challenge Is Given

But what was the strange thing that was happening on the
Philistine side of the valley! A huge man was standing, well in
front of the line of Philistine soldiers. He was shouting across at
King Saul and the soldiers of Israel. His great voice echoed and
re-echoed between the low hills as he roared:

"I defy the armies of Israel! What can they do against the
mighty Philistines? Send out your bravest, biggest man, your
best soldier, and I will fight him here. If he can win against
me and kill me, the Philistine army will surrender to you. But if
I kill him, our army will claim victory over you."

The giant's boasting challenge brought fear to the hearts of
all the Hebrew soldiers. Saul himself stood aghast. Great soldier
though he was, he, too, was frightened.

Nor was this the first morning when the towering man had
swaggered out and repeated his loud, defiant shout. By now the
Hebrews knew who he was—the terrible giant of whom they
had often heard the wildest rumors. People had said he was over
nine feet tall! He would stand head and shoulders above King
Saul himself. And there he was, clad in metal armor from

---

[1] Two different forms of this ancient legend are found in the Bible. The story
here is based on I Samuel 17: 1-11, 33-53 (with some verses omitted that are
not in the Septuagint or Greek translation).

head to foot. A helmet of brass covered his head, and he held a heavy shield before his body. His javelin seemed as long as a weaver's beam.[2]

Each time the giant strode down the hillside, the men in Saul's army stood as though nailed to the ground. The terrifying silence was broken only by the frightened whispers that went around among the Hebrew soldiers. "Who would be bold enough or foolish enough to meet this monstrous man in single combat, especially when victory or defeat for our whole army depends upon it! If only there were still a Samson on the Hebrew side! Who but a Samson would dare to fight with this Philistine giant!"

The Challenge Is Accepted

Saul and David stood side by side in silence. They looked across the valley, each thinking his own thoughts but saying nothing. Finally David spoke up: "If no one else will go and risk his life and our army's fortune to meet this bragging giant, let me go, O king!" Perhaps David was almost as greatly surprised at the sound of his own voice when he spoke as was Saul, beside whose tall figure he seemed but a dwarf.

"What!" exclaimed Saul in astonishment. "You cannot go against this brawny Philistine with his huge spear and his heavy coat of mail! You could not get past his shield-bearer who goes before him. You are only a lad, and that giant has been trained as a soldier from his youth up."

Humbled by the king's rebuff, David remained calm, as he said: "But this does not require a seasoned warrior, O king." David already had a plan in his mind. "When I kept my father's sheep on the hills of Bethlehem, I often had to fight singlehanded against enemies as fierce and frightening as this giant. When a lion—or a bear—used to come out of the woods to take one of our lambs, I went after him with the only weapon that a shepherd can use."

For several minutes the king said nothing. Should he accept David's offer? Or should he be annoyed at this foolhardy youth?

---

[2] The name Goliath has been intentionally omitted from this chapter. In II Samuel 21: 19, it is said that Elhanan killed the giant Goliath. In I Samuel 17, the giant is referred to simply as "the Philistine" without giving him a name, except in two verses (I Samuel 17: 4 and 23) where the name may have been added by a later writer. There may well have been several such giants.

A PHILISTINE GIANT

The designs have been taken from paintings found in the ruins of Philistine cities.
From The Foundations of Bible History: Joshua, Judges, *by*
John Garstang. Used by permission.

Saul turned his head toward David and looked at him long and steadily. David waited and watched the changing expressions which passed over the king's face.

At length the older man laid his hand on David's shoulder. "Go," he said, "and may Yahweh be with you." Then Saul offered David his own armor and shield and sword, and sent him back to his tent to make ready for the contest. But the king's equipment proved not only too large for David's slight figure; it was much too heavy and hindered his movements. He had already planned the kind of attack he would make on the giant, and this called for quick, agile action, with legs and arms free to move swiftly. So he carried the armor back to the king, and laid the pieces down on the ground before him. "I have never tried using such armor, and I cannot use it now."

David then returned to his tent and soon reappeared in his usual simple tunic with his shepherd's staff in one hand and his sling in the other. He walked down to the brook which flowed through the valley, and carefully selected five smooth stones, each a little smaller than a man's fist. These he put in his shepherd's bag that he slung over his shoulder. He then stepped forth in front of the line of Hebrew soldiers, and started down the hillside.

The Outcome

The soldiers on both sides watched him intently. The Philistines shouted mockingly: "What kind of game is this stripling going to play?" The men of Israel stared half in hope and half in despair, showing by their grim silence their doubt and yet their admiration for the young man's quiet courage.

When the Philistine giant caught sight of David, his contempt knew no bounds. Angrily he shouted: "Do you think I am a dog, that you send this boy out with a stick and stones to fight me?" And he cursed David in the name of Dagon, his God, and roared: "Come on, little champion, and I will give your flesh to the birds of the air and to the beasts of the field!"

The Philistine soldiers kept up their jeering, yelling more loudly with each step David took toward them. The giant, too, continued his taunts and threats. Leaving his shield-bearer behind, he came slowly toward David, puffing and bellowing,

wearing himself out with his fury, pushing his great hulk along,
burdened as he was with the weight of heavy armor. While the
two were still many yards apart, the giant stopped, pushed back
his helmet in order to cool his sweating face, and stood glaring
at his small rival.

David saw his chance, quickly took a stone from his bag, put
it in his sling, spun it around his head a few times and hurled it
straight at the giant's head. His aim was perfect. Long practice
with the sling had made it so. His stone went straight to its

EGYPTIAN MUSICIANS PLAYING LYRES

mark, hitting the exposed forehead of the giant who, without knowing what had struck him, reeled and fell forward, stunned. Before the Philistine could recover his senses, before the shield-bearer or any of the Philistine soldiers could make a move, David rushed forward, picked up the giant's huge sword which had fallen to the ground, and struck a final blow to finish his victim.

This sudden and unexpected end of the affair in the valley had different effects upon the two armies on the opposite hillsides. The Philistines, horrified at the quick turn of events which had laid low their giant, stood dumb and speechless, their loud taunts dying in their throats. They knew only too well that the shameful defeat of their champion at the hands of the young Hebrew meant that their whole army must, according to the terms they had offered, surrender at once. In another moment, thinking to save themselves from such disgrace, they turned and ran for their lives in disorderly retreat.

In the same instant, at a command from Saul, the men of Israel with loud shouts started in hot pursuit. They poured down from the hillside and across the stream, and charged up the opposite hill behind the frantic, fleeing Philistines. Saul's men did not give up their chase until the enemy was driven clear back across their border in scattered confusion.

Saul stood by his tent and watched his own soldiers' victorious pursuit. Assured of their success, he turned to an attendant and commanded that he bring David to him.

As the younger man approached, Saul welcomed him as the hero of the day and said: "You have done well, my lad. You have saved us all from what might have been defeat for us. Now you must not think of going back to your home in Bethlehem, but you must stay with me and my army from this time on." David received the king's words in silence, not knowing what answer to give.

The Beginning of a Friendship

Beside the king stood his son, Jonathan, who had done nothing this time for Israel's victory. In Jonathan's eyes David saw a look of admiration as great, he felt, as that which he himself held for the king's son.

As they left the field on the way back to Gibeah, Jonathan

took David's arm and led him aside from the path which the king and his attendants were following. "What is Jonathan going to do?" thought David. Would he be jealous, this young man who had been the hero of all the soldiers up to this time? How would he feel, now that another had taken his place as the favorite among the men in the army, and as the one whom the king had praised so highly? But Jonathan soon put David at his ease—for "Jonathan loved him as his own soul."

When the two were alone, Jonathan looked straight and lovingly into David's eyes, and taking both his hands into his own, he said with deep feeling, "You and I must be friends forever." Then, following a custom of the time, Jonathan said: "Let us make a covenant of friendship together," and he took off his armor and gave it to David, together with his sword and bow. David in return gave Jonathan his sling shot and bag of stones.

This was the beginning of one of the most famous friendships in all history, and from that day on, the two young men remained completely devoted to each other, and neither one ever forgot the solemn pledge of friendship they made there where no one else could hear.

12

From Hero to Fugitive

NEWS OF THE SLAYING of the Philistine giant spread rapidly throughout the country. By the time King Saul, and his son Jonathan, and David—the great hero of the hour—were ready to begin their march back home to Gibeah, the Hebrew people in the villages round about were waiting in curious excitement to welcome them back. Crowds gathered along the streets in every town through which the returning soldiers passed. Women shaking tambourines and clanging cymbals came dancing out of their homes, and singing as they danced. They had a new song for this new exciting occasion and they sang it over and over.[1]

> Saul has slain his thousands
> And David his tens of thousands.

King Saul was truly proud of his young armor-bearer. Saul knew well that David's brave and skillful deed had saved them in a frightening crisis. Yet after hearing this song of praise over and over in town after town, King Saul grew irritated by the great honor being given David. "They give David tens of thousands," he said, "and I get only thousands! What more can he now have but the kingdom itself?" Thus once more there grew in King Saul's mind the old fear of having a rival.

A Love Affair

After this victorious combat with the giant, the three men and their soldiers returned to King Saul's fortress town of Gibeah. During the following days, as Jonathan and David talked over their experiences together, they almost forgot that they were not blood brothers, they became such close friends. There was also a sister in the royal family who became extremely fond of the

---

[1] The stories in this chapter are based on I Samuel 18: 1-12, 20-29; 19: 1-18a; 20: 1-42; 22: 1-23.

young hero. To tell the truth, Michal quickly fell in love with David. She watched for ways to show him special kindnesses. Naturally David was pleased to receive so much attention from the king's beautiful daughter, and it was easy for him to return love to her.

Apparently King Saul was too absorbed in his own problems to notice the developing courtship. But the attendants in the palace were well aware of what was happening, and were afraid that trouble might be in store for the young daughter. Finally, one of these servants told the king that David and his daughter Michal were in love, and was surprised to find that the king seemed pleased.

But if the king showed outward pleasure over this report, he was really thinking dark thoughts. His mind was uncomfortably divided toward David. Saul loved the young man for his courage and skill and for his charming friendliness, but Saul still feared David as one who might some day take his throne from him. What should Saul do about this love affair? Should he encourage it or should he put a stop to it? Finally he decided to encourage it. "Perhaps it would be better to admit David into the family and so have him near me where I can keep an eye on his movements, rather than to send him away to fight in the army."

King Saul, therefore, told one of his servants to go secretly to David with this message: "The king respects you as a valuable leader in his service. He knows of the strong friendship between you and Jonathan, his son, and how greatly Michal, his daughter, loves you. The king would be pleased to grant his daughter to you in marriage."

The Dowry Asked For

The servant did as he was told and later reported to Saul the answer David had given. "Though I could see that the young man loves your daughter, O king, he said that he, a poor man, could never hope to be the king's son-in-law, for he could not afford to pay the dowry[2] required to marry a princess."

When King Saul heard David's reply, he said to the servant:

---

2 A dowry was a payment made by the husband to the father of the bride.

"Go back and tell the young man that I shall not require the usual dowry from him. I shall ask a gift which I know he can give. Tell him to go out and kill a hundred more Philistines. If he does that and brings me back proof that he has done it, he may have my daughter." By this requirement, King Saul secretly hoped that the venture might even cost David his life.

David, of course, did not know the vicious plan that was in the king's mind. He thought merely that his courage was once more being tested. David really loved Michal enough anyway to risk his life in order to have her as his wife. It was generous of the king, he felt, to make it possible for him, in spite of his being poor, to marry the princess.

At once David made preparations for the difficult and dangerous task required of him. With some of the best fighting men under his command, he started for the nearest Philistine garrison. His raid proved successful, and he returned in triumph to King Saul to present the gruesome trophies of his victory. Although Saul was surprised and even alarmed at David's prompt success, the king could not renounce his promise. So he gave his daughter Michal to David in marriage, and all the royal family merrily celebrated the wedding.

A Murderous Plan

King Saul, however, could not long cover his disappointment. His fear of David's popularity began to change into hatred. Saul had spells when he went about the house raving wildly. The family said, "An evil spirit has overpowered him." A rumor spread that one day the king tried to spear David while he was playing on his harp. But as Saul lifted his spear to hurl it, David skillfully slipped aside and fled from the room.

Not long after this, so it was said, the king made still another effort to kill his son-in-law. Michal and David had settled down together in a house of their own that stood beside the city wall. Indeed one of its windows was high up in the wall itself.

King Saul secretly sent two messengers to the house. He commanded them, saying, "Watch David unceasingly all through the night. Do not let him escape. In the morning when he comes out of the house, capture him."

But someone warned Michal of her husband's danger. When

A FEAST GIVEN BY A NOBLEMAN OF MEGIDDO
He may have lived during David's lifetime.

she told David, he could not believe the rumor. He tried to dismiss Michal's fears by calling them "nothing but a woman's fancies." But Michal insisted: "If you do not save your life tonight, you will be a dead man tomorrow." She planned the one way he could escape without being seen by the king's guards. In the darkness of the middle of the night, she let David down by a rope through the window in the city wall. Once on the ground below and outside the city wall, David ran for a hiding place in the woods to wait for further instructions.

Michal was sure that the men waiting outside would come to the door in the morning and demand David's surrender. So she prepared for them. As soon as David was gone, she found the image of their family god. She put it into David's bed and wrapped some goat's hair on its head to resemble a man's hair and covered the rest of the image with the bedclothes.[3]

As expected, the men came into the house in the morning. Michal took them to the door of David's room, pointed to what appeared to be a man sleeping in the bed. "He is sick," she said, and they believed her and carried back this word to the king.

The report made Saul angry and more determined than ever to capture David. He sent the men straight back to the house with the order: "Bring David to me in his bed." When they returned to David's house, they quickly discovered Michal's trick, which they reported at once to Saul.

---

[3] Such images, called "teraphim," were probably common in Hebrew households of that time. They represented the family gods.

The king was furious, went striding to his daughter's house and said to her hotly: "Why did you try to deceive me and help my enemy to escape?" Michal was afraid of her father's anger. To save herself she put the blame on David, saying: "He made me do it, and he threatened my life if I would not help him escape." Michal knew now that her father's insane jealousy would stop at nothing.

A Lonely-Fugitive

Meanwhile, David was a fugitive, fleeing for his life. Only a short time before, he had been the king's favorite, and had been taken into Saul's own family. He was enjoying the friendship and respect of all the leaders of his nation. But now he must wander alone, with the king's men hunting him as if he were a wild animal. What would his many friends think of the sudden turn of his fortune? What would the Hebrew people say— those who, but a little while ago, had sung his praises when he had returned with the king from the victory? "Ah!" he thought bitterly, "that was the real beginning of my trouble. Their song was the spark that kindled in Saul's mind this jealous fury against me."

Deepest of all in David's thought must have been the question: "How will Jonathan take my misfortune?" David could not forget his dearest friend and the covenant the two of them had made together. David was sure that Jonathan would be grieved to learn of his father's blind rage which had made David's departure necessary, even as David himself would be saddened if any harm should come to his friend. But what could Jonathan do now? If he should try to help David, the king's fury might be turned against his own son. David half hoped that Jonathan would not take such a risk, yet he could not put away a secret desire that Jonathan might be able to do something for his friend in trouble, and make it possible for him to return home.

For a few days, David remained in the neighborhood of Gibeah, keeping himself hidden from view in out-of-the-way places, hoping that he might hear the good news that the king had changed his mind. Perhaps, thought David, it is only one of Saul's attacks of illness that makes him send the officers to Michal's house. Yet David feared the worst, and when no word reached him from Michal, he decided to take refuge farther away where he would be less likely to be found. Indeed he fled to Ramah, where Samuel lived.

Jonathan's Friendship Is Tested

In the meantime, Jonathan knew nothing of what had happened. When Michal told him that David had been obliged to flee in the middle of the night, Jonathan was greatly surprised. He could not believe it was true that his father had tried so openly to make away with David.

Jonathan was not content until he had searched the countryside and had found his friend. When the two met, Jonathan's first question was, "Why have you come out here, David? I have missed you and, ever since Michal told me, I have been looking for you everywhere. Michal is much alarmed for your safety, but I do not think my father really intends to harm you."

"I am here, Jonathan, because your father is determined to kill me. But what is my guilt, Jonathan? What wrong have I ever done your father that he is seeking my life?"

"You have done nothing, David. You are not going to be put to death! My father never does anything, either great or small, without letting me know. Why should he hide such a thing as this from me? No! No! It cannot be!"

"It is because your father knows that you and I are such close friends, Jonathan. He has said to himself: 'Jonathan must not know this because it would grieve him.' But as surely as our God lives and as surely as you live, Jonathan, there is only a step between me and death!"

"What can I do for you, David? I am willing to do anything you ask. I would risk my own life for you."

David was ready with a plan of action. "Tomorrow," he said, "the festival of the new moon will begin, when I should be at the king's table. If your father misses me, tell him that you gave me permission to go to my home in Bethlehem to be present with my family when they hold a yearly sacrifice. If the king accepts your word, I shall be satisfied that he no longer wishes to kill me. But if he becomes angry, then we shall know that his mind is still disturbed and he still plans to harm me."

Both young men were silent for a moment. Then David said

thoughtfully, "But how am I going to find out how your father feels toward me? It will not be safe for you to come again to see me, for he may send someone to follow you and find me."

This time Jonathan suggested a plan. "I shall come back to this place in three days, pretending to practice in the field with my bow and arrow. I shall bring a lad with me to pick up the arrows I shoot. You hide yourself behind that little hill over there so that you will not be seen. I will shoot three arrows toward this side of the hill as though I were shooting at a mark on it. Then I'll send the boy after the arrows. If I say to him, 'See, the arrows are on this side of you,' then you will know that it will be safe for you to come back home with me. But if I tell the boy, 'See, the arrows are beyond you,' then you may be sure that your life is not safe in Gibeah."

When the king and his family gathered next day for the feast, Jonathan sat at the table next to his father, while David's seat was vacant. The king said nothing about it during that meal, but the next day, when David was again expected to be present, Saul asked: "Why has not David been here, neither yesterday nor today?" He was pretending to Jonathan that he did not know why David had gone away, so that his son would not suspect his plot against David. Jonathan, just as innocently, gave the excuse which he and David had arranged to make.

Immediately the king's anger flared up. He shouted: "Your mother was a bad woman and you are like her. You should be ashamed to be so intimate with that miserable young upstart, the son of Jesse! Don't you know that as long as he is alive, you will never become king? Go now and bring him here, for he must die!"

Jonathan rose from the table in hot anger and refused to eat more because his father had insulted him. He stood stubbornly before his father and pleaded for his friend: "Why should he be put to death? What has he done?" On hearing this, Saul's face grew red with rage. He wildly seized his spear which had been standing in the corner near him, and hurled it at his son. But Jonathan was too quick to be caught. He had observed his father's hand reaching for the spear and he sprang up from his place before it started its mad course toward him. He rushed from the room to escape any further outburst.

The next morning Jonathan went out, as he had arranged with David, taking his bow and arrows, and accompanied by a boy. Arriving at the appointed spot where David was hiding behind a low hill, Jonathan carried out the rest of their plan. But to show David how serious his danger was, Jonathan added, as the boy started for the arrows, a warning intended for his friend in hiding: "Make haste, don't delay, waste no time."

Jonathan's boy gathered up the arrows and brought them again to his master. Jonathan gave the arrows back to the lad, saying, "Return with them to the city and leave me alone a while."

As soon as the lad was gone David came out of his hiding place, and ran to Jonathan. He knelt low at Jonathan's feet, but Jonathan made David stand up, and he threw his arms about him. They kissed each other, and wept on each other's shoulders. And again they pledged each other their love.

A Fugitive Once More

Finally the two men parted—sad and heavy-hearted. Jonathan walked slowly up the hill and back to his fortress home to tell his sister Michal. David turned southward to wander alone, he knew not where.

EGYPTIAN PIPERS AND A HARPIST

Would he ever see Jonathan again? Or Michal? She had saved his life—but what for? To live away from her? How could he? Why had he ever supposed he could make love to a king's daughter? If only he could go back home to Bethlehem! If only he could talk once more with his father or mother or one of his sisters or brothers! But would they understand? Would they blame him? Would they be afraid to take him in? Then he would have to move on farther south secretly—on and on—wandering and hiding. How long? Oh, how long would this loneliness last? David's mind worked anxiously hour after hour as he trudged along.

With his farewell to Jonathan that afternoon, there began another life for David the son of Jesse. There was to be hunger in it and loneliness and hardship. Try as hard as he could to disguise himself, someone sooner or later was sure to recognize him. Word would then be promptly sent back to King Saul, and fresh detachments would hurry out to capture the fugitive.

When these spying troops failed to find David, those who were suspected of having helped him to escape were sometimes captured in his place. Some even were killed for having given him shelter or food.

Finally, David entered the very valley where in his boyhood he had often tended his flocks. In an afternoon, he could have walked across the valley and home to Bethlehem. The lonely hillsides he knew so well seemed friendly to him. Oh, what a relief it would be to be within those walls again! How beautiful the old home seemed to him now as he pictured his father and his brothers there.

But, far away as he was from Gibeah, David knew that he was not safe. King Saul probably had his spies even there in the southland. David would not endanger his family or his neighbors by showing himself or asking any kindness of them whatever.

Fortunately he found on the hillside an ideal hiding place. It was a cave large enough to hold several hundred men and yet with an opening on the hillside that was almost hidden from sight by outcropping rocks and bushes. The opening was also small enough so that a half dozen men with swords could protect themselves from an attack.

But some shepherd must have seen this stranger wandering

over the pastures and recognized him, and he must have reported his presence to the family and to the townsfolk. For it was not long before David's brothers and men of his father's clan came out to the Cave of Adullam to see him.

Now these people of Bethlehem, like so many others in the southland, had long disliked Saul. They had never been happy over his having been made their king. When they heard the story from David's own lips of how Saul had turned against their hero, they really hated Saul.

As the days passed, more men came to the cave and asked for the privilege of joining David's band. It seemed as though every one who came had some kind of special difficulty. Either he had gotten into debt and was afraid he might be sold as a slave or he had a grievance of some kind against somebody. All these gathered around David and urged him to lead them in a revolt against King Saul. Even a priest of Yahweh, named Abiathar, came—a man who had been doing duty in a shrine in a small town where David had once taken refuge. He told David how King Saul had destroyed their shrine, how the other priests had been killed because they had helped David to escape, and how he alone had escaped alive. "Let me join your band, David," he said, "I have brought the *ephod* with me and whenever you need to inquire of Yahweh what to do, I shall be near to make the prayers." From that time on for many years this faithful Abiathar followed David wherever he went.[4]

So David who, but a short while before, had been a lonely fugitive wandering without companions soon found himself occupying the Cave of Adullam with about four hundred restless and disgruntled men who were all bent on supporting him against Saul. It was no easy task for David to hold these rough men back from doing rash things. They kept urging him to gather more men and to go forth and fight Saul. If only David would lead the revolt, they would make him king instead of Saul. But David was not willing. All he wanted was to keep out of danger and to wait. For he realized that to fight King Saul would

---

[4] Some students of the Bible think that this priest Abiathar may have been the person who first wrote down the stories of David's adventures which are now in our Bible; for Abiathar was perhaps the only man with David who could read and write.

mean fighting also his son Jonathan. David could not forget his promise to his friend. David remembered that Jonathan had risked his life for him. If David had to choose now between being king and being true to his friend, David decided to be loyal to his friend.

13

More Adventures as a Fugitive

Now THAT DAVID HAD FLED into the southland of Judah, he might have expected that Saul's soldiers would no longer bother to pursue him. But this did not prove to be the case.

Although King Saul claimed Judah as part of his kingdom, yet he had never been able to spare the soldiers needed to conquer it fully. Consequently, in the south David found another enemy to face. The Philistines still ruled a number of large walled cities, and from these cities their soldiers made frequent raids against other towns to seize food and supplies from the thrifty farmers and landowners.

A Rescue and a Brief Reward

One day not long after Abiathar, the priest, had come to David, a tired, excited runner appeared at David's camp beside the Cave of Adullam, asking for help for the near-by town of Keilah. "The Philistines are fighting against Keilah," he shouted breathlessly. "They are robbing the threshing floors! They are taking all the grain we have threshed for the winter. Come quickly and help us! There are no soldiers from King Saul to defend us!"

David's first thought was to go to the help of the people of Keilah, since Saul's forces were not at hand to be feared. But could David risk a battle with the Philistines? Could his untrained band of followers, now grown to six hundred men, have any chance against a well-armed force of trained warriors? David was not sure what might be the best course to follow. He therefore decided to consult the *ephod* which Abiathar had brought with him.

"Shall I make an attack against the Philistines at Keilah?" he asked the priest. Abiathar went to the *ephod* with the question,

1 The stories in this chapter are based on I Samuel 23: 1-14; 26: 1-25; 27: 1-12; 28: 1-2; 29: 1-11.

111

and returned with the answer: "Yes, go and save Keilah." But when David told his men of his plan, they were afraid and said: "Why, we are just a band of outlaws. How dare we attempt a battle against the mighty Philistines?"

David went a second time to Abiathar and asked: "Is it certain that we can defeat the Philistines?" The answer came: "Yes, go down to Keilah." Encouraged by this second assurance, David went back to his men and told them of his decision, and they, seeing how confident David was of victory, started out loyally behind him.

The Philistines had been watching only for the approach of Saul's soldiers from the north. They were unaware of the presence of David's newly gathered force in the neighborhood to the south, and were taken completely by surprise when the fierce, yelling band from Adullam suddenly fell upon them. The Philistines were defeated almost before they knew what had happened, and Keilah was saved. When David and his men entered the town, they were greeted joyfully by its grateful people.

How welcome to David was the opportunity to settle down and live again in a house in a town! So much better than wandering as a fugitive and an outlaw, or living in the cave at Adullam! But such comfort did not last long.

Word of what had happened soon reached the ears of Saul, who for some time had not known where David was. The king was delighted and boasted: "Ah! David is now my prisoner, caught in a walled city from which he cannot escape! Now I can capture him, as I could not do when he was roving around the country!"

The king himself, with a strong force, set out immediately from Gibeah to attack Keilah. David had expected this to happen, but he had hoped for a little more time before Saul's arrival. David wanted time to win the loyalty of the townspeople and also time to train the men sufficiently to withstand the king's attack. How he wished that the rumor were untrue that Saul was already on his way!

In his uncertainty, David went again to Abiathar, his priest, to consult the *ephod*. Two questions troubled him, and he asked these of the priest. "Will Saul really come here, as I have heard he would?" The answer was, "Yes, he will come." Then David asked: "Will the men of Keilah deliver me into Saul's hands?" The answer again was "Yes."

This was what David feared would happen. Yet he realized how natural it was for the people of Keilah, now that their king was on his way, to give their loyalty to him. After all it would be dangerous for them to risk King Saul's anger or oppose the power of his army. Although the people of Keilah had asked this small band of outlaws to rescue them from the Philistines, they had not yet been won to the idea of revolting against King Saul.

David understood this well. Disappointed though he was, he and his men left the city, and again took up the roving life of fugitives. They could not even return to the Cave of Adullam, since that hiding place was now well known to all. They went, therefore, farther south to hide wherever they could in the wide, lonely stretches of hilly country west of the Dead Sea.

King Saul Is Once More on the Trail

Once more King Saul had failed to capture David when success seemed almost sure. So he returned to Gibeah, leaving only a few men to continue following the fugitive.

David, of course, kept constantly on the move, and had his own spies watching for the approach of the king's men, for he well knew that King Saul would not easily give up the chase.

Later when word reached Gibeah that David's hiding place had again been found, King Saul set out once more on the trail, this time taking with him Abner, his chief captain, and three thousand men. Into the wild and barren mountains of southern Judah they came. Exactly where David and his band of six hundred men were they did not know, for these outlaws flitted about from one place to another like birds flying from branch to branch. The king's men would go to find them in one place, and when they arrived, the roving band would be twenty or thirty miles farther south or eastward in the rugged hills near the Dead Sea.

One evening Saul's army set up camp on a hillside a few miles southeast of Hebron. They believed that David's band was not far off; yet King Saul did not know that that very night his enemies were camping in the deep woods on the opposite side of the same valley. David and his men kept themselves well hidden from the sight of their pursuers.

In fact, David and his men were watching the king's men all the afternoon as they set up camp. And when the darkness of night fell over the valley, the outlaws could see the whole camp clearly outlined by the light of their campfires. It was an exciting experience for David's men, and he had some difficulty persuading them to rest quietly for the night and to wait until morning to decide their next step.

When all his men were finally asleep, David was still about. With two companions he walked farther up the mountain where the outlook was open. There on a rock they stood in silence, watching the flickering lights across the valley and wondering what they should do. With David was Ahimelech, his chief captain, and Abishai, his loyal young nephew.

King Saul and His Men Sleep

Suddenly David had an idea. "Who will go with me tonight into King Saul's camp?" he said, turning first to Ahimelech, his brave captain. Ahimelech shook his head. He could see no sense in such a risk. David then turned to his nephew and asked "Will you go with me, Abishai?" and Abishai answered, "I will go with you, uncle, wherever you say."

In the darkness the two started out, cautiously making their way down through the gorge in the valley and up the opposite hill. They found Saul's sentries off guard, evidently fearing no attack from the valley side of their camp. Stealthily David and Abishai crept through the camp until they came to the very place where the king lay sleeping. They knew his tent by the spear which had been thrust into the ground outside it. Beside the spear was a jug of water.

Abishai, thinking that David had planned this secret journey for the purpose of killing Saul, whispered in the darkness: "Yahweh, our God, has put your enemy into your power. Let me kill him now. It would take only one stroke of the spear to do it."

"No. Do not kill him," whispered David. "After all, he is the king, Yahweh's royal servant, whom we must not harm. When

Saul's time comes to die, Yahweh will strike him dead or he will be killed in battle. But we must not take it into our hands to kill him." Abishai was astonished and wondered just what David was going to do, now that they had risked their lives to come to the king's camp.

"Take Saul's spear," whispered David, "and the jug of water that is here by his tent, and let us go." This seemed to Abishai a very unimportant thing to do, and not worth all the danger to which they had exposed themselves. But he did as David wished, for he was sure that his leader must have a plan in mind.

David and his nephew got away as quickly and as quietly as possible. No man saw them and no one knew of their being there. Neither did anyone wake up.

Shoutings across the Valley

By early morning the two were back once more in their own camp. Again David climbed to the high rock on the hillside. Over on the other side of the valley he could see the lights around the king's camp. No one seemed to be moving about. Evidently the men were still asleep. David cupped his hands and shouted with all his might, "Ho! King Saul! Ho! Abner! Why do you not answer?"

Abner was the first to be wakened. He ran out of his tent and looked about. He called angrily across the valley: "Who are you that cries to the king?" Not knowing that David was anywhere near, Abner thought this rude shouting was being done by one of his own soldiers who ought to be punished for disturbing the king's sleep so early in the morning.

David's voice came back through the morning air: "Are you not a brave man, Abner? Who is like you in Israel! Why have you not kept watch over your lord, the king?"

Abner was furious when he heard this taunt, not yet knowing who it was that made it. David had more to say, now that he knew Abner was listening. "Someone has just been in your camp. He could have harmed your king. You have not been on guard. You have slept at your post of duty. You deserve to die for this. Where is the king's spear? Who of you can find the jug of water that was at his head?"

By this time Saul had also awakened and heard the shouting from the other hill. He recognized David's voice. Astonished, he cried: "Is that your voice, my son, David?"

"Yes, my lord, O king," replied David, "it is my voice. Why does my lord pursue his servant? What have I done to you? What evil have I been guilty of?"

It was difficult, shouting across the great space between the camps, but the quiet of the early morning helped the sound to carry. David became bolder, now that Saul had called him by the old familiar name "my son." He walked down to the valley and halfway up the hill nearer to the king's camp. He wished to say many things to Saul without being in danger of capture by the angry Abner.

David was now within easy calling distance of the king, where he could speak at greater length and be understood. "Let the king hear what his servant has to say. If it is Yahweh our God who has turned you against me, let me offer a sacrifice to set right whatever wrong I have done. But if evil men have told lies about me and made you pursue me, let them be cursed. They have driven me from Israel — away from the presence of Yahweh to a strange land where I cannot serve him. It is as though they said to me 'Go, serve other gods.' I beg you, O king, let me not meet my end here, away from Yahweh. Your seeking my life, O king, is like a vulture pursuing a partridge in the mountains." [2]

Saul was deeply impressed by David's appeal. It made him realize that he had wronged his young friend and son-in-law. "I have sinned against you, my son David!" Saul confessed tenderly. "Come back and I will do you no further harm, because you spared my life when you might have taken it as I slept. I have acted like a fool. I have made a horrible mistake!"

David was surprised to hear the king's honest confession, but he was much pleased. "Here is your spear, O king," he said, holding it high above his head. "Let one of your men come and get it. As I have valued your life too highly this day to take it, so may my life be protected and so may I be delivered from my troubles."

Saul now felt very kindly toward David. He called back:

---

[2] The reference to the vulture is found in the Septuagint and is omitted in the King James translation.

THE GORGE OF ADULLAM
David and his men hid in these caves.

"May you be blessed, my son David. I know that you will do well in all you undertake. Farewell!"

A short while after this, King Saul ordered his men to break up camp and they returned to his fortress capital of Gibeah.

A Dangerous Game of Deceit

David wanted to accept the king's invitation to return to Gibeah, but he feared that the king might quickly forget his generous promise, for he still often had attacks of melancholy.

"If I am not on my guard all the time," thought David to himself, "I shall yet meet my end at the hand of Saul. I must go somewhere, even out of Judah, for I know I shall never be safe from Saul's pursuit as long as I remain in the country over which he has any control." David puzzled long and carefully over his problem before making his plans for his next move.

Finally he thought of a strange and dangerous course of action. He might take refuge in one of the Philistine cities. "Where else can I go," thought David, "than to the Philistines? King Saul would not dare send his soldiers into their territory to capture me." Yes; it would be a dangerous course to follow. It would seem unpatriotic to the people of Israel for him to go over to the side of his people's old enemies. But where else could he go? He must either go to Philistia where he might be safe, or remain in his own country where he would be continually pursued and where he would always run the risk of capture.

His mind was made up. David gave the order to his band of six hundred to make ready to cross the border into the land of the Philistines. He had decided that one of the five kings of the Philistines, King Achish of Gath, whose city lay nearest to Adullam, would be the easiest man to approach.

David's men were astonished. They trembled at the thought. The risk of meeting the Philistines might be even more dangerous than that of facing Saul's warriors. But their loyalty to David was unwavering. They were ready to go anywhere with him.

For David the adventure was not altogether a leap into the dark, for he had carefully framed a plan to use in dealing with the Philistines. It was going to be a dangerous game to play, and it would require constant caution and shrewd, cunning maneuvers on his part, but in his desperate situation he was ready to take the risk. He would pretend to be altogether friendly with the Philistines, giving them the impression that he was a deserter from his own people. But all the while he would be careful not to take active part with the Philistines in their war against Israel.

Messengers were sent ahead to Gath to explain to King Achish that David and his men were coming to make terms with him and not to fight against him. The Philistine king was surprised at this unexpected offer of David's, although he had heard rumors of trouble between David and King Saul. King Achish knew, too, that these men whom David had trained were brave and able soldiers, for he had heard about their victory over the Philistine forces that had tried to raid Keilah. Perhaps it had been part of this very king's own army which had suffered that crushing defeat. "How wonderful it would be," King Achish thought, "to have this force of skilled fighters on my side against the Israelites! They know the enemies' country, and they know the Israelite ways of fighting better than do my generals. How terrified the Israelites will be to find one of their own best generals waging war against them!"

David's request was too good an opportunity for Achish to refuse, and when David himself came to talk with him, the Philistine king was completely won over by the apparent sincerity of the attractive young leader. King Achish welcomed David and his men to join his army at Gath. To be sure, some of the Philistine officers were not so easily persuaded to accept this new ally. They were suspicious of the sudden change of attitude on the part of this man who had so recently fought against them, and who had more than once distinguished himself in his leadership of Israel's forces. But King Achish would not listen to their objections, for he had made up his mind to accept David as a friend.

In his new position, however difficult it might be, David found a splendid opportunity to study at first hand the weapons, the organization, and the tactics of the Philistine army. During the first months of his league with King Achish, David knew that he must make a good impression upon the Philistine leader, while at the same time he must try not to bring harm to the Israelites. He therefore made many secret attacks on various desert tribes, other than the Israelites, which were constantly raiding the country of Judah. When carrying out these attacks, David showed no mercy to these enemies. He saw to it that these foreign barbarians, as he called them, were completely wiped out, so that none would be left who might tell King Achish what had happened.

When David returned to the king's headquarters and the king would ask him, 'Where have you made a raid today?" David would answer, "In the south of Judah and in the desert where the Kenites live." But he would not tell who it was he had attacked. Sometimes he even sent secretly to the people of Judah gifts from the spoils which he captured.

David's New Move in His Game of Deceit

David realized that this deceitful game he was playing with King Achish could not long continue, for the king would soon learn what was really happening and turn against him. David, therefore, carefully planned another move. He must arrange somehow to be transferred to a place far removed from the city of Gath in order to be safe from the king's constant observation.

David, therefore, went to King Achish and proposed: "If I have pleased you with my services, O king, will you not give me a place in one of your cities in the south where I may settle down?" And David added flatteringly: "It is too great an honor for me, your humble servant, to remain here in your royal city with you." King Achish fell easily into David's trap and obliged him at once by giving him Ziklag, a Philistine city far in the south.

But David's troubles did not cease when he reached the distant city of Ziklag where he thought he would be safe from the Philistines' sight. News soon reached him there that the five kings of the Philistines, including his own friend, King Achish, were planning to join all their forces in the greatest all-out attack against Israel which they had yet attempted. It was to be their final push which would overcome the Israelites once and for all and drive them completely from the land.

It was indeed alarming news for David. "What can I do now?" he thought. "King Achish will surely expect me and my men to fight on the Philistines' side against King Saul and my own people!" David was not surprised, therefore, when a messenger from King Achish summoned him to Gath. David knew how embarrassing it was going to be to face the Philistine king, yet he could not refuse to go to Gath.

David's difficulty grew worse when he appeared before the king, and heard his command: "Of course, you and your men are going out with my army to battle against Israel."

It was a difficult moment for David. He answered vaguely without making any real promise. "It is well, O king. You will soon see what I, your servant, will do." King Achish took his answer as an agreement that he would fight with the Philistines, and he replied gratefully: "If you do well, I shall honor you by making you captain of my bodyguard as long as you live."

David, of course, was still hoping that he might find a way out of his perplexity without letting King Achish know just how he felt. But he had to pretend that he was glad and willing to go into the battle. The Philistines' plans were already complete by the time David came to Gath, and almost before he knew it he found himself and his men marching northward in company with the Philistine forces.

Would he, after all, be compelled to do this terrible thing, to fight against his own country and people? Here he was, on the road toward the border of Israel, every step taking him nearer and nearer to a battle which he would give almost anything to avoid fighting.

The Philistine Generals Suspect David

The Philistine armies were already nearing the Plain of Esdraelon when it happened — the fortunate event which saved David from the very thing he feared. Some of the Philistine generals, who had never favored the king's decision to welcome David to their side, came to Achish and protested against having David and his men march with them. "What are these Hebrews doing here?" they muttered angrily. Achish, who had trusted David from the very beginning and all through the time he had been in Philistine territory, anxiously tried to defend him now.

"You ought to know," he said, "that this is the former servant of Saul, and that he has been with me for a long time. He has always been faithful. I have never found any fault with him since he deserted the Israelites and came over to our side."

But the Philistine generals became more angry and insisted: "Make this man return to the place to which you appointed him. We do not want him to go into battle with us. How do we know that he will not change sides again and be reconciled to his former master and fight for him against us?"

Crestfallen, King Achish finally went to David to try to explain the embarrassing situation in which he found himself. As politely and humbly as he knew how, the king said: "David, my friend, you know that I have always been pleased with what you have done as long as you have been with us. But I must tell you now that my generals do not want you to go into this battle with them. It will be better for you to go quietly back to Ziklag so as not to displease them. They are stubborn men and will not change their minds."

David could hardly conceal his feeling of relief at this welcome news, but he did not dare to appear too eager to leave. So he pretended to be hurt and disappointed at the turn of events. "What have I done to deserve this discharge? And what have you found wrong in me during all this time I have been with you, that I may not go out now to fight against the enemies of my lord, the king?"

Once more King Achish had to repeat sadly the decision which his generals had forced him to make. "For my part, I know that you are blameless. But these generals have insisted that you must not go into the battle with them. I beg you, therefore, to start out early tomorrow morning and go back to Ziklag."

With a heart lighter than it had been for many months, David went his way southward with his men. He grieved only at the thought that the Philistines whom he was leaving behind would soon join in battle against King Saul and the army of Israel. David could not help wishing that he might do something to help his people, if only to warn them of the Philistines' intentions and their elaborate plans. If only he could tell them some of the things he had learned about the Philistines' tactics, the habits of their generals and soldiers, and the organization of their fighting forces! But he was in no position now to do anything except retire to Ziklag.

14

"Thy Glory, O Israel, Is Slain!"

THE PHILISTINE KINGS WERE CONFIDENT that soon they would finally defeat their Hebrew enemies. They would conquer the entire land of Canaan and build an empire on the ruins of the
Kingdom of Israel. To this end King Achish of Gath and an army
of thousands of well-trained and well-armed soldiers were marching northward along the Mediterranean plains. They were planning to attack King Saul's kingdom from the north where his
defenses were weak. They were counting also on help from the
garrison they had established in the fortress city of Beth-shan
near the eastern end of the Plain of Esdraelon.

King Saul, on hearing rumors of this alarming advance of the
Philistines, tried his best to prepare for the coming battle. He
mustered as large a force as he possibly could and put each of
his three sons, including Jonathan, in command of a large bat-
talion. Together they took a position on the western slope of
Mount Gilboa. From there they had a wide view of the Plain
of Esdraelon and of the valley through which they expected the
Philistines to advance.

But the Hebrew king soon realized how weak their position
was. If they were not able to hold it, there would be little chance
of retreat, especially with the Philistine soldiers so near-by in
the fortress city of Beth-shan.[1]

A Séance with a Witch

What could King Saul do? It was too late to make other plans.
His usual courage and coolness in the face of battle was giving
way to fright. How he wished now, in his great danger, that he
might ask a priest to consult the *ephod* for him! But no priest
was near. In his own savage jealousy, Saul had slain all the

---

[1] The stories in this chapter are based on I Samuel 28: 3-25; 31: 1-13; II Samuel
1: 1-27.

priests of Nob except Abiathar, who had escaped with the *ephod* and was now in exile with David. If only Yahweh would come in a dream and tell him what to do! But no dream came. Trembling with fear, Saul went to the prophets, those wild, dancing, singing patriots who had often been able to turn the tide of war by filling the soldiers with a frenzied spirit of resistance so much needed in battle. But the few prophets who were at hand had also come to see the hopelessness of their king's position, and their courage, too, had ebbed away.

In his plight, he thought of those witches who claimed to be able to call up the ghosts of the dead. King Saul had formerly believed that these witches were frauds. As king he had forbidden them to carry on their strange practices. But now he was not so sure. What if they really could bring up the ghosts of the dead! What if one of these witches could bring the prophet Samuel back! What would Saul not give to have a word with his old friend!

To the poor, frightened king, it was a last forlorn hope. All other means had failed to give him the help he needed in his desperate hour. He decided to take the risk. He secretly asked two of his attendants if they knew of any one of these witches who was still in the country. Yes, they told him, there was one in the little village of Endor just a few miles away.

So when nighttime came, King Saul changed his clothes and disguised himself as a common soldier. Under the cover of darkness he and his two companions set out on foot for the home of the witch. On their arrival, Saul said to the woman, "I want you to bring back from the dead the person whom I shall name so that I may talk with him." Although the witch did not recognize her visitor as the king, yet she was cautious. It was well to ask a few questions. "Don't you know that King Saul has driven out all witches from the country?" she asked slyly. "Why do you come to lay a trap for me?"

But Saul was not to be refused. He quieted her fears by giving her his promise, "No harm or punishment will come to you if you will do as I tell you." Thus assured, the woman admitted Saul and his companions to her house and invited them to sit down. "Whom do you want me to bring up for you?" she asked.

Trying not to appear too eager, Saul said, "Bring up the prophet Samuel for me." The woman eyed him suspiciously. She knew that King Saul was in the neighborhood with his army, and at the mention of Samuel's name, she suddenly sensed her danger and cried out in great alarm: "Why have you deceived me? You yourself are Saul, the king!" Saul again assured her, "Do not be afraid. I will not harm you."

He noticed then that the woman began to act strangely, as though she were in a trance, peering about the room and then staring wildly toward one corner of the earthen floor. "What do you see?" asked Saul. "I see a spirit coming up out of the ground," she cried.

"What does he look like?" inquired Saul anxiously. "He looks like an old man, wearing a robe," she answered.

Saul was thoroughly frightened, and trembling he threw himself down on the floor. He hoped for a favorable answer to his great question, but he feared the worst. He saw nothing, of course — the woman only pretended to see the ghost of Samuel. But Saul wished to take no chances; he must be reverent, he thought, in the presence of the great Samuel. In his excited state, Saul was ready to believe anything the woman might tell him. He thought he heard a voice speaking to him — a thin, hollow, far-away sound: "Why have you disturbed me, to bring me back here?" Saul cringed.

"Samuel, my lord, I am in sore trouble. The Philistines have come to make war against me, and I can get no answer from Yahweh, our God, to tell me what I should do. He has forsaken me. I have waited for a dream, but none came. I have asked the prophets, but they have no answer. So I have called you to advise me what to do."

Again came that weak, croaking voice, as though from a great distance — more like a hoarse whisper of wind than like a human voice. "Why do you ask me, when Yahweh has left you and has turned against you? He will give the army of Israel into the hands of the Philistines."

At these words, Saul fell headlong to the floor in a faint. His fear had overcome him. He was weak, for he had eaten nothing all that day and night. The woman quickly prepared some food

and persuaded him to eat. Somewhat revived but still weak and
hardly able to walk, the king went back to his camp, half carried
by his attendants.

Blood on the Slopes of Gilboa

The next day the unfortunate Saul, still unstrung by the fearful experience of the night, had to lead his army against the
powerful Philistine forces. There could be little hope for men
whose leader was already sure of defeat, although he tried not
to show his despair.

The large Philistine army ran up the mountainside to meet the
Israelites. Saul's terrified men fought back heroically for a while
but soon realized how impossibly trapped they were. They tried
to flee, but most of the men fell slain on the slopes of the mountain. Only a few succeeded in getting away. It was the worst
defeat that Saul's armies had suffered. Among those who perished were all three of King Saul's sons — even Jonathan, David's
beloved friend.

During the flight, King Saul himself was wounded. He realized
that the Philistine archers were close behind him, and he was
greatly distressed. He said to his armor-bearer, "Draw your sword
and thrust it through me. If these barbarous Philistines capture
me they will abuse me." But the armor-bearer could not bring
himself to do such a thing. He was too afraid.

So the poor, half-crazed king took his own sword and fell
upon it. When his armor-bearer saw that his lord the king was
dead, he likewise fell upon his sword and died with his king. "So
King Saul died, and his armor-bearer, and thousands of his men,
that same day died together."

The Philistines pursued those who escaped, following them
even to the other side of the River Jordan.

The next day some of the Philistines came to the field of battle to strip the bodies of the slain. On finding the bodies of King
Saul and of his three sons, they carried out one of the savage
customs of ancient warfare. They stripped the bodies of their
armor and carried them triumphantly through the streets of Beth-
shan to show to all the grim trophies of their victory. They even
took them and paraded them before the images of their gods.
Finally they hung the naked bodies on the city wall of Beth-shan.

THE TAKING OF A WALLED CITY IN CANAAN

This picture was made for the Egyptian Pharaoh Rameses II.
From The Foundations of Bible History: Joshua, Judges, *by John Garstang. Used by permission.*

The Loyal Townsmen of Jabesh-Gilead

News of this defeat and of King Saul's death reached the little town of Jabesh-Gilead east of the Jordan River, and brought great sorrow. This town had never forgotten how, many years before Saul had come to their rescue when the Ammonites were besieging them. The people there had always been proud of King Saul. In loyal gratitude for his heroic service to them, a band of men of Jabesh-Gilead immediately set out for Beth-shan. It was a full night's march, but they brought back the king's body and the bodies of his three sons from the city wall of Beth-shan and gave them a decent burial near their city. There the men mourned and fasted for seven days.

Word Is Carried Also to David

All the while David and his band of fugitives were many miles to the south in Ziklag. Finally, several days after the battle, a man came running into the camp who claimed that he had been on the battlefield and had even seen King Saul fall upon his sword. The messenger told the whole sad story. David was overcome with grief. He tore his clothes and wept and refused to eat. His men also mourned for King Saul and for Jonathan his son and for all the people of Israel.

So deeply moved was David that his poetic soul found words so expressive of deep sorrow that they have been preserved through these thirty centuries, as one of the great elegies on death to be found in the world's literature. Some of the verses describe the tender feelings of friendship as few lines from ancient times have done.

> Thy glory, O Israel, is slain upon thy high places!
> How have the mighty fallen!
> Ye mountains of Gilboa,
> Let there be no dew or rain upon you, fields of death.
> For there the shield of the mighty was dropped.
> Saul and Jonathan, the loved and the lovely;
> As in life, so in death, they were not divided.
> They were swifter than eagles,
> They were stronger than lions.
> How are the mighty fallen!
> In the midst of the battle!

Jonathan is slain upon the high places.
I am grieved for you, my brother Jonathan.
Greatly beloved have you been to me,
And your love to me was wonderful,
Greater than the love of women.
How are the mighty fallen
And the weapons of war perished!

15

Two Contenders for the Kingdom

THE DEATH OF SAUL and of his three sons on Mount Gilboa might have brought the complete ruin of Israel. Instead the tragedy made possible the birth of a greater nation. Saul had failed and his kingdom seemed hopelessly lost, but he had laid a foundation on which others could build. He had taught the Hebrew tribes that they could stand together in the face of danger and attack.[1]

Ishbaal Is Crowned King in the North

With Saul's death, Abner, the general of Saul's armies, was in no mood to surrender completely. He gathered up the broken remains of his shattered troops and retreated across the Jordan River and found refuge in the town of Mahanaim, about ten miles southeast of Jabesh-Gilead. This part of the country had never seemed important to the Philistines, so that the refugees were safe from attack. There Abner set up a kind of temporary capital and began his search for a new king. The only surviving son of Saul was a young man named Ishbaal, and Abner set him up as "king of Israel."

David Is Chosen King in the South

All this happened while David was far away in southern Philistine territory, governing the town of Ziklag as a puppet ruler under Achish, the Philistine king of Gath. David had heard the news of the tragic battle on Mount Gilboa, and he had sincerely and deeply mourned the loss of King Saul; and the death of Jonathan, his friend, broke his heart. Yet David was not a man to give up in despair. He determined to act and in some way help to bring order out of the great confusion. He did not yet

---

[1] The stories in this chapter are based on II Samuel 2; 3; 4; 5: 1-5; and 23: 13-17.

know that Abner had set up the young Ishbaal as king. David knew only that someone must step forth as the new leader before it was too late, and it seemed to him that he was the man in the best position to do so. His hard experiences as an outlaw had taught him many valuable lessons in dealing with men and with difficult situations. His adventures as a pretended ally of the Philistine King Achish had given him knowledge of the Philistines' methods of warfare, of their strengths and their weaknesses.

As he thought over his plan of action, David decided that it would be best for him first of all to take charge of affairs in Judah, his own home country. During all of Saul's reign, the territory of the tribe of Judah had never been as fully under the control of Saul as had been the tribes of the north. It was divided from the rest, in fact, by a strip of territory, still occupied by Canaanites, reaching from the Jordan River in an almost unbroken line westward to the Mediterranean, and including the City of Jerusalem.

It was in Judah that David had lived during the days when Saul was hunting him. During his years there as a fugitive, David had made many friends among the people. Perhaps now that Saul was dead, they would be willing to accept him as their leader. Should he try? It seemed to him that there was no one else ready or able to take control.

His first step was to go to Abiathar, the old priest who was still with him. David talked over his plan with the priest, asking him finally to consult the *ephod* in order to know whether or not this was the right course to follow. The answer was: "Yes, go to Hebron."

At once David gathered his men together, with their families and possessions, and left Ziklag. They went to the largest city of Judah, named Hebron, which was about thirty miles to the east of Ziklag. Here David was immediately welcomed by the chief men of Hebron, who recognized him as the very man they needed as leader. They called together representatives from the towns around. A few days later they met and chose David as the king of Judah. As reckoned by our calendar, David became king about the year 1000 B.C.E.

We do not know whether or not the Philistine king, Achish, favored this new move on the part of David. It may be that he approved the plan and regarded David as his own representative to govern the territory of Judah as a Philistine province.

One of David's first acts as king of Judah was to send a message to the people of Jabesh-Gilead, whose men had risked their lives to rescue Saul's body and the bodies of his sons from the walls of Beth-shan and to give them a decent burial.

"May the blessing of Yahweh our God be upon you, because you have shown this kindness unto your lord. I wish that I too might reward you for this noble act. Be strong and brave! Although Saul, your king, is dead, the people of Judah have just anointed me king over them."

"What a generous gesture on David's part!" thought some. But others said, "He is merely making a strong hint that he himself should be considered the proper man to follow Saul as king of Israel."

Seven Years' War between the Contenders

It was not until after this that David heard that Abner had made Ishbaal king over what was left of Israel. This changed the situation, for now David could not urge the people of the north to make him their king when they already had a king. Yet David was ambitious to have the two kingdoms — Israel in the north and Judah in the south — united into one nation. Ishbaal had a similar ambition. The trouble was that both of the men were ambitious to become the one great king of this larger nation.

Each man had his own army and his own chief commander. Abner was the general of Ishbaal's army and Joab was David's chief commander. While Saul was living, these two men had fought side by side as friends. But now fears and suspicions grew between the two armies. One quarrel and murder led to another and poisoned the feelings of the people in the two kingdoms against each other. Seven years of cruel civil war followed, during which Ishbaal was bent on making Judah a part of his kingdom, while David was hoping and trying just as vigorously to unite the north and the south into one nation under his kingship.

Ishbaal proved to be the weaker of the two men. Like his father, Saul, he was jealous of rivalry, and he soon turned against Abner, the only really capable leader in the north. Abner then realized that he had made a mistake when he supported this

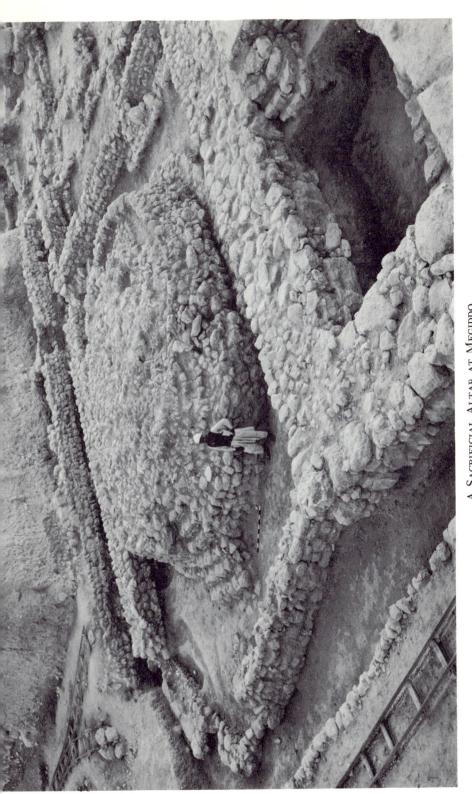

A Sacrificial Altar at Megiddo

David may have been crowned at an altar like this one unearthed in the ruins of Megiddo.

weakling as king of Israel. The only other thing to do, thought Abner, is to make the more able David the king of Israel in Ishbaal's place. He therefore sent a message to David, saying: "If you will make an agreement with me, I will bring the people of Israel to your side."

Pleased with the message, David sent back word to Abner: "I will be glad to talk things over with you on one condition. Bring Michal, Saul's daughter, with you. I paid the dowry required for her and she is my rightful wife."

But during the years that had passed since the time when David had fled from Gibeah, Michal had married another man. So Abner had to take Michal by force from Phaltiel, her new husband, who did not relish giving up his beautiful princess. Indeed, it was rumored that he followed Michal a good part of the journey to Hebron, weeping all the way. Finally Abner had to order him to go back home alone, and Phaltiel obeyed.

So David's desire for Michal was satisfied. Perhaps having King Saul's daughter as one of his wives added strength to his claim to the kingship. At any rate, David, the new king of Judah, and Abner, general of the northern armies, agreed to work together to make Israel and Judah into one nation and David was to be king of both north and south.

In the end, David was accepted by the people of the north, but not until further tragedies had occurred, in which both Abner and Ishbaal were assassinated. With these two men removed and no other capable leaders left in the north, the people of Israel were ready to offer the kingship of their land to David. Soon the elders of northern Israel appeared in Hebron to anoint David as their king.

The Philistines Resist David's Growing Power

At last David's great hope was fulfilled, but he was wise enough to know that the hardest task of his life still lay before him — to weld these two kingdoms into one, so that all the people would think of themselves as citizens of a single nation. Fortunately David was still a young enough man — hardly forty years old — to be undaunted by the difficulties which lay ahead of him.

Not only must the new king manage to set up a firm government for Israel and Judah, but he must be able to protect and defend it from attacks by enemy countries. The neighboring countries would not wish to see a strong power rising so near them, and they would doubtless do everything they could to prevent this possibility.

Chief among these enemies were the Philistines, who had so completely defeated Saul, and who even now held much of the territory which had belonged to Israel. As long as David was content to rule the territory of Judah as a sort of Philistine province, they had been willing to keep the peace with him. They may even have been pleased to have David carry on civil war with Israel's broken state, as he had seemed to be doing all through Ishbaal's reign. This would relieve the Philistines from having to send soldiers to keep Israel from becoming strong again. But now that David had become the independent ruler of a united kingdom, the Philistines recognized him as their enemy who must be conquered if the country were ever to become part of the Philistine empire.

The Philistines acted quickly. Before David could even go to the north country to be welcomed by the people of Israel as their new king, Philistine forces marched southward and took a position in a valley just north of Bethlehem. Thus, they thought, they would be able to keep a close watch on David and could prevent him from making any move to assemble the combined forces of Israel and Judah against them.

Once more David was forced to go into hiding in the Cave of Adullam where he had so often taken refuge from Saul's spies. David's faithful company of fighting men was increased by many soldiers who came to him from all parts of Judah. From this hiding place, his men carried on a kind of guerrilla warfare, moving out secretly at night and striking the enemy suddenly from behind their lines. Adventurous warriors kept the Philistines frightened continually by making surprise raids—here, there, and everywhere.

These tactics succeeded in accomplishing just what David hoped they would, for the Philistines withdrew farther and farther to the west and south. Before long it was possible for David to make his way safely into the north country where he could

gather the forces of Israel's remaining fighting men. He combined these with his own well-trained army from Judah, and
launched a great drive against the enemy.

David Honors Three Brave Men

During this period of guerrilla fighting, an incident occurred,
the story of which has been a favorite to all admirers of David.

One of his guerrilla bands had just returned from a dangerous
exploit. The day was hot and breathless. David was terribly
thirsty. His thoughts went back to his boyhood days in Bethlehem, and he said longingly: "Oh that I might have a drink of
the cool, fresh water of the deep well that is by the gate of
Bethlehem!" He knew, of course, that it was an idle wish, for
the Philistines had their garrison near that very spot, guarding
the city and keeping a sharp watch for him. It seemed unthink-
able that anyone could approach the well without being captured by the enemy.

Yet, as soon as David had spoken, three of his men started
out to get the water. They knew they were risking their lives
by trying to penetrate the Philistine lines. Yet they felt that
their king's wish was a command. They succeeded in reaching
the well and brought back the water and offered it to the king.

David was so deeply touched by their deed of devotion for
him that he could not bring himself to drink the water when it
was handed to him. "No," he said, with deep feeling, "I cannot
bear to take this from you. It would be like drinking your blood,
for you have risked your lives for my sake." He paused for a
moment. He looked into the faces of the three men. He saw in
them the affectionate loyalty he had once seen in the face of
Jonathan. Finally David found the words he wanted to say
"God forbid that I accept this gift, my friends. It belongs to
God as an offering of blood." So he took the pitcher in his hand
and poured the water out upon the ground, just as the priest was
accustomed to do with the blood of animals slain on an altar.
To David it was a token of his gratitude for the self-sacrificing
devotion of his men. The men who saw it loved him all the more.

16

The New Capital

WITH THE GREATEST of his country's enemies no longer a serious threat, and with the smaller nations around them also quiet, the young king was free to organize a widespread kingdom without fear of interruption. He started on his task hopefully, planning each step with great care. He talked matters over with his trusted advisers, especially with Joab, the commander of his army, and with Abiathar, his faithful friend and priest. Often these comrades of his could offer wise suggestions which David might not think of by himself.[1]

A Bold Plan Is Conceived

So it was that one day the king talked with Joab. "My lord," said the general, "do you not think that it would be wise to establish your headquarters and your royal court in the north country? Hebron is rather far south. And the territory of Israel is so much larger than Judah. I have heard some of the elders in the north talking of this, and I believe that it would please the larger number of people there to have their king living among them. Saul always kept his home in Gibeah, and perhaps the fortress of Saul, which the Philistines destroyed, could be rebuilt and made the capital of your great kingdom."

"I too have thought of that, Joab," replied the king. "But you know, as I do, that if I moved to the north country, my own people in Judah might be envious, just as the people of Israel are jealous of their southern brothers while I remain here among them."

"But where can you place your capital, then?" asked Joab.

"You cannot stay here in Hebron. You say you cannot go to Gibeah. What other place is there that does not belong to one of the tribes?"

---

[1] The story of this chapter is based on II Samuel 5: 6-10.

When David spoke again, he looked steadily at Joab with what seemed almost an accusing gaze. "I am surprised, Joab," he said in even tones, "that you, a warrior, and one who has led many campaigns against cities and villages of our land, have not thought of the only place that would make a perfect capital . . ." Before David could name the place, Joab rushed to speak: "The city of the Jebusites! Is that what you mean? I had thought of that myself once, but what a fortress it is! There it has stood through all these many, many years, protected by massive stone walls built upon steep, rocky cliffs. A perfect capital! But impossible to capture!"

Difficulties Are Acknowledged

The "city of the Jebusites" was the ancient city of Urusalim, whose king, at the time of the beginning of our story, had been Ebed-Hepa. It had indeed stood there, unconquered through all the years, too heavily fortified for any of the Hebrew tribes to attempt to capture. Jerusalem (as it was later called), and the strip of country extending from it to the Mediterranean, had continued to be a barrier between Israel's tribes in the north and Judah in the south. Not even the Philistines had ever ventured to attack the mighty stronghold. Few Hebrews had dared to think of its ever being conquered. David had passed within sight of it many a time during his years of wandering as a fugitive from Saul. But the more he thought about Jerusalem, the more convinced he became that it was the perfect capital for his kingdom and that now was the time to attempt its conquest.

"Joab," he said quietly, hardly heeding the general's words of misgiving, "take some of your best men secretly and go to Jerusalem. Examine its walls and its defenses. We must capture it. It belongs to no one of the tribes. It is the only place in which to set up our capital."

In spite of David's words, Joab lost none of his anxiety over the prospect of taking Jerusalem. He went on to describe what seemed to him the hopeless task which the king proposed. "You see, my lord," he said, "three sides of the city are protected by broad, towering walls on top of steep hills that rise straight up from the valleys round about. The fourth side has a great double defense wall which no enemy has ever penetrated. I have been

close to those walls to see how solid they are. We have no bat-
tering-rams to pierce them. Not even the Philistines, with all
their war machines and mighty army, ever felt equal to such an
undertaking. You know, those Jebusites have a saying that the
blind and the lame in the city are enough to keep anyone from
entering it."

David remained unmoved by Joab's speech. "Yes," he said,
"I have heard that saying, too, and I have seen those great stone
walls, just as you have. But we *must* have that fortress — no other
will do. We must take that strip of land which now keeps Israel
and Judah from joining their boundaries. The city cannot have a
very great force of defenders. Perhaps they are too confident that
their high stone walls will save them. Surely you should be able
to find a way to get inside the walls, and, once we are inside, the
city will be ours. Go, Joab; find the weak point in their defenses.
Come back and tell me when you are ready to undertake the attack. There must be a way.

Spies Study the Situation

"I go, my lord, and may my mission be successful."

David had many things to occupy his mind while Joab was
absent, and the time went rapidly by. The king talked with
others of his friends and advisers about some of the great plans

A PROCESSION OF EGYPTIAN WOMEN
Playing tambourines and dancing.

he was forming for his kingdom. Abiathar, the priest, was one with whom he had many long conversations, for already David was thinking about having a house of God in the city which he hoped would be his capital.

"Good Abiathar," he said one day to the old priest, "what would you think of going to Kirjath-jearim, where the ark of Yahweh has been resting ever since the Philistines sent it back from their country when the great plagues broke out? We are now in possession of that place again, and we ought to bring the ark back into the midst of our country and our people. When I have built a new capital, shall we not make it the center of the people's religion as well as of their government and the royal house?"

Abiathar's eyes gleamed with satisfaction when he heard these words of his king. "O king," he said, "it would be well to recover the ark once more and to put it where all the people may come near to it. But where will you bring it? Where is this new capital to be of which you speak? Shall it be here in Hebron or will you go into the country of Israel where Saul dwelt as king?"

It seemed too soon to tell Abiathar his plans about Jerusalem, for the priest might not approve of this dangerous undertaking, so David merely said: "When I have decided where the best place is, I shall come to you again, Abiathar, and you shall help me make plans for bringing the ark to it." The priest seemed satisfied with this and bade the king good-by.

At this moment, a page came, announcing that Joab waited to see the king.

"Hail, O king," said Joab as he entered the room where David sat. "I have just returned from the Jebusite city with my men. We went all around its walls, and examined all the defenses most carefully. I believe, sir, that we have found the very place to enter the city. Outside the wall on the east, there is a large spring which furnishes the city's water supply. From that spring a tunnel leads through the rock foundation of the city wall, to a shaft which opens higher up inside the walls. Water is lifted up through this shaft into the city. The shaft is large enough for a man to climb up. We could send a small group of picked men secretly into the tunnel and up into the city through the shaft. They would thus take the people inside the city by com-

A HORNED ALTAR
Found at Megiddo.

plete surprise, and the whole population could be easily thrown into confusion. Our men would draw the guards off the walls by raising great excitement when they entered. Then it would be a simple matter for the rest of our army, which would be waiting on the north side of the city, to storm the unguarded walls and capture the fortress."

The Attack Is Carried Out

David listened with growing excitement as Joab unfolded his plan. "An excellent strategy, my brave Joab!" he cried. "Prepare to lead the expedition. Choose your most daring men to climb up the shaft. Gather an army to scale the wall by the north gate of the city. I myself will lead them. And when you send us word that your men have entered the tunnel, we shall watch for signs that the guards have withdrawn from the top of the wall. Then we will make a quick scaling of the walls, open the north gate, and take the city."

It took but a short time for Joab to make the preparations. A large army was gathered from both Israel and Judah. The march to Jerusalem was accomplished. Without the Jebusites' knowledge, the plan was put into operation. It worked perfectly. The city was taken with but little violence and bloodshed just as David had hoped. The Jebusites made little resistance. David made easy terms with them. They chose to surrender rather than to fight. They cared more for their city and for their homes than for freedom.

The Hebrews were jubilant. They paraded the streets shouting and singing, "Hail to our great King David!" Their musicians played on their harps and clanged their cymbals and shook their tambourines as the people danced.

Wives and children from Hebron and whole families related to the soldiers soon came and settled in the city alongside the Jebusites. Workmen repaired buildings that had been damaged in the fighting, and new ones were built. The conquerors grew proud of their mighty fortress and of the wonderful old city that they now called their own. They soon gave it a new name—"The City of David." For they knew it was his bold strategy that had won it; but David himself declared that it was Yahweh, their God, who had led them to victory.

17

The Ark of Yahweh

WITH THE TAKING OF THE City of Jerusalem, the renown of the people of Israel grew by leaps and bounds. This wise stroke ended the ambitions of the Philistines for an empire in Canaan. They still held some strong points on the Plain of Esdraelon, the most important of which were Megiddo and Beth-shan. David, however, succeeded finally in driving the Philistines out of these strongholds and thus wrested the entire plain from their hands. He destroyed the walls of Beth-shan on which the bodies of King Saul and Jonathan had been hung in disgrace. Its temples were plundered of all their riches and the entire city was burned in a blazing fire. By this time David was in control of practically the whole land of Canaan, leaving only the Phoenicians along the coast toward the north as strong neighbors. But the Phoenicians did not threaten David's kingdom, for they were more peaceable than the Philistines, and they were more interested in carrying on sea trade on the Mediterranean than in conquering their neighbors. Indeed one of the kings of a Phoenician city, the king of Tyre, sent messengers to David, greeting him as the new ruler of all Israel.[1]

A Royal Palace for the King

King David was ambitious to build in Jerusalem a royal palace that would really be impressive, but he was not skilled in the art of building. Nor were his countrymen. The king of Tyre, on the other hand, had many fine architects in his royal city of Tyre. His country was rich in its cedar forests. His lumbermen were accustomed to send cedar logs on large carts many miles across country. There were also many skilled masons.

---

[1] The story of this chapter is based on II Samuel 5: 11, 12; 6: 1-19; 8: 1; Psalms 24: 7-10. For mention of Hiram as King of Tyre here (II Samuel 5: 11) see note 3 of Chapter 21 below.

143

The king of Tyre promised to send cedar logs and stones and carpenters and masons, while David probably agreed to protect the caravans that passed through his kingdom bringing goods from the east to Tyre for the Phoenician sea trade. Thus the friendly agreement between the two kings brought advantage to both. Soon supplies of building materials and great numbers of Phoenician workmen arrived in Jerusalem to build for King David a royal house on the Hill of Zion—a palace such as no king of Israel had ever known.

A Place Where Yahweh Might Dwell

But in King David's plan there was still another part which had not been carried out. This was the bringing of the ark of Yahweh into the capital city. Abiathar the priest was delighted when King David sent for him, but he could scarcely believe what his eyes saw when he entered the city.

"Your Majesty," he said when in the king's presence, "this is a happy day for me! Yahweh our God has truly been good to us in giving us this great fortress city. On walking up the hill I was amazed at the height and thickness of the old walls. Your courage was greater than mine. I wonder that you could even have imagined you could take the city."

"Yes, Abiathar, Yahweh has indeed been good to us. What is even more wonderful to me is that the city fell into our hands with almost no fighting or bloodshed. Few of our men and few of the Jebusites were lost in action."

"May Yahweh be praised!" exclaimed Abiathar. "It is more wonderful than a dream! And to think that already you have begun building a palace fit for the king of such a nation as yours. I am filled with surprise at the sight of the many workmen I see going to and fro, each busy with his own assigned task."

"But, good Abiathar, I am not yet satisfied. I shall have a palace soon, it is true. But there is no house for Yahweh. We must bring the ark of Yahweh here. You remember we talked of this before."

"It will be the greatest day of my life, O king, when I see the ark of Yahweh brought into this royal city. Then we can feel that Yahweh himself will stay here with us in this city he has given us."

"I hope, Abiathar, that some day we can build a temple for Yahweh alongside my palace. A large building and grand in its beauty—a temple worthy of our great God. But we cannot wait for that. For the time being the holy place for the ark will have to be simply a large tent such as our ancestors used to have in the desert."

"Do not let the lack of a grand house for Yahweh disturb you, O king. What is important is that the ark should be here in the capital of our nation." Then the old man turned his head and looked dreamily out a window. He spoke slowly and softly.

"Not long ago a story was told me of the pioneer days in Canaan. When our ancestors first entered this land from the desert, a small sanctuary was built in the town of Shiloh where the ark rested for many years. To that shrine the scattered tribes used to send their representatives to do honor to Yahweh. Shiloh was a center to which all might come in time of danger or when they wished to celebrate a victory. In fact, the ark was at Shiloh when the Philistines first captured it and destroyed the shrine. How long ago that was! Long before I was born! And I am now an old man!"

"Yes, Abiathar, I too have heard stories of those terrible days. But we shall see better times soon for our people and for the ark. Some day there will be in Jerusalem a temple larger and more beautiful than the shrine at Shiloh. To this temple our people will come from all parts of our great kingdom. They will come especially on the holy days of the year. To be sure they will still have their smaller shrines near their homes, where daily and weekly they may come to sacrifice to the God of Israel. But here in this capital city, they will come to rejoice on special occasions at a temple which will be for all."

The First Journey of the Ark

With great care the king himself took charge of preparations for the journey of the ark from Kirjath-jearim and for its reception in Jerusalem. It was to be a great triumphal procession, and nothing must happen to mar the perfect carrying out of every detail of this most solemn and memorable undertaking. As David and his people believed, it would be like welcoming Yahweh himself to his rightful place in the new national capital;

for where the ark was, there was Yahweh's earthly dwelling place.

The story is told that David made two attempts to bring the ark to Jerusalem, the first of which failed because of an unfortunate accident.

According to this story, King David, with a large company of chosen people, went to the town of Kirjath-jearim to get the ark. They had a new cart built especially for the occasion, and chose a pair of perfect oxen to draw it. While the trumpets blew and people played on harps and timbrels and clanged their cymbals and sang, the ark was placed upon the cart and the procession started down the hill, with Uzzah in charge of the driving.

Unfortunately, at one place along the way, one of the oxen stumbled, and Uzzah reached out his hand to keep the sacred box from falling. It is said that Uzzah immediately fell dead. All who saw this tragedy declared that Yahweh had struck Uzzah dead. But why? Some people said it was because Uzzah touched the sacred ark. Others said it was because he had presumed to protect Yahweh himself, who really needed none to protect him. Even King David became afraid of Yahweh that day and ordered the procession stopped and the ark carried aside and put away in the house of Obed-Edom, who was a Philistine but a worshiper of Yahweh.

Some think that what really happened was that Uzzah, overcome by the great excitement and exertion of the day's celebration, fell dead from a heart attack. Others suggest that he was perhaps accidentally run over by the heavy wheels of the cart and·met his death at the side of the road. In any case, in those ancient days, the grim mishap was taken to mean that Yahweh was displeased for some reason unknown to the people, and that he showed it by bringing Uzzah to his early death.

The story of this incident, as it was repeated by ancient story-tellers, has given us a figure of speech, used to this very day. A person who appears to be over-anxious to take God's part in the management of the world is sometimes called "an Uzzah, who tries to steady the ark of God."

The Second Procession to Jerusalem

It was a solemn and awe-struck procession that returned to Jerusalem without the ark. King David and Abiathar the priest

A CANAANITE WOMAN OF RANK

An ivory plaque found in the ruins of Megiddo.
The eyes are made of Phoenician colored glass.

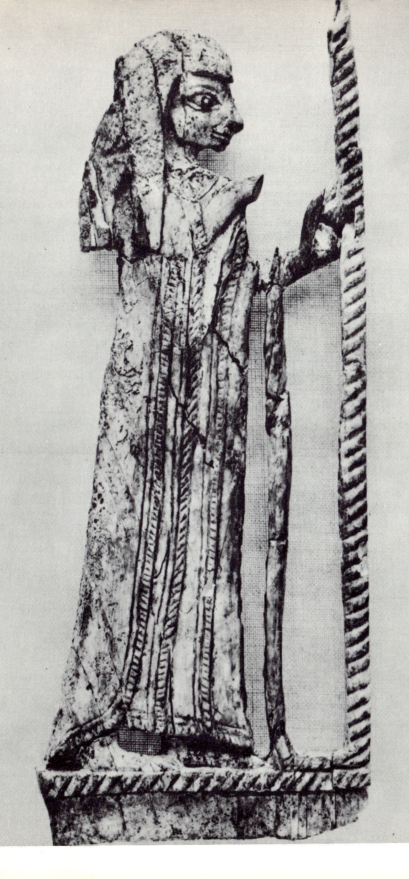

waited. They said little. Even they had been overcome with fear by what seeemed an undeserved punishment.

When three months had passed, however, a messenger came to the king, saying: "The family of Obed-Edom were never so happy and prosperous as they have been since the ark was put into their house." David took this to mean that Yahweh's anger had passed and that the ark might now be safely brought into Jerusalem.

So the king again took charge of preparations for the journey and for its reception in the capital city. Again a large company of pilgrims started forth from Jerusalem. Again the ark was placed upon a cart and driven by two oxen. A brilliant and joyful procession accompanied the sacred box every step of the way. Trumpets were blown whenever they neared a town along the way. The king led the procession. They marched and sang in wild excitement to the musical accompaniment of harps and drums and cymbals. So filled with gladness and gratitude was King David that he stopped the procession many times and offered sacrifices of thanksgiving to Yahweh on altars that had been built by the side of the road.

It was an unforgettable hour when at last the procession stood before the closed gates of the walled City of Jerusalem. It may be that one of the songs sung by the people on that triumphal morning was a psalm composed by the poet-king. Some think that Psalm 24:7-10 gives the very words chanted as the ark approached the gates. We can imagine the scene that took place, as the procession paused just outside the great closed gates and sang:

> Lift up your heads, O ye gates,
> And be ye lifted up, ye everlasting doors,
> That the King of Glory may come in!

From inside the city came the question, sung by a chorus waiting in front of the tent:

> Who is this King of Glory?

At once the throng outside made answer in clear, ringing tones:

> Yahweh, strong and mighty,
> Yahweh, mighty in battle!

Then after a hushed pause, the people outside the gate repeated their song:

> Lift up your heads, O ye gates,
> Yea, lift them up, ye ancient doors,
> That the King of Glory may come in!

The chorus inside responded as before:

> Who is this King of Glory?

And the loud, echoing song of the waiting crowds outside the still closed gate gave answer once more:

> Yahweh, the God of hosts,
> He is the King of Glory!

Silently the gates swung open and the jubilant procession swept into the city. First came the men carrying the precious ark. Then came the king himself, dancing behind the ark. Straight to the tent moved the singing and dancing throng. In the great open space before the tent they gathered as the ark was carried in and set down behind the curtains.

Then came the climax of the great occasion. Oxen and sheep were brought to the stone altar that stood before the tent. There these animals were slain and their blood poured out on the altar and the flesh roasted as offerings of thanksgiving to Yahweh. When the sacrifices were completed, David spoke a prayer of thanksgiving and blessed all the people.

Then as a friendly and happy ending, the king gave out to everyone in the entire crowd, both to the men and to the women, a cake of bread and a portion of the flesh roasted on the altar and a cake of raisins.

So all the people departed—everyone to his own house—in a satisfied and thankful mood.

18

Power, Luxury, and Tragedy

The Power

All the while that King David worked to improve the City of
Jerusalem, he continued his wars against neighboring countries.
He was ambitious not only to strengthen his defenses, but also
to enlarge his kingdom. This meant drafting larger numbers of
men for his armies and raising larger taxes to support them. No
longer was David content merely to make the neighboring
countries his allies. He was set upon subduing them and weakening their power to make war on Israel. It was, therefore, not only
the Philistines whom he drove out of the land or made subject to
him. He also sent his armies across the Jordan. He defeated
the Ammonites, and the Moabites, and the people of Edom to
the south. He even sent his men northward beyond the Sea of
Galilee and on up to Damascus and placed garrisons of his
soldiers in parts of Syria.[1]

Sometimes on these raids his armies captured horses and
chariots by the hundreds. Sometimes they captured large numbers of foot soldiers and marched them off into Canaan to be
sold or given away as slaves. These captives from the wars were
used to cut down the trees of the forests. They quarried stones.
They built roads and houses and fortifications. Sometimes the
soldiers also brought back from their wars many valuable articles
of brass and of silver and of gold. This booty was brought to
Jerusalem to bring luxury into the king's own palace, or was sold
or given away to other families who were in the special favor of
the court. Regular yearly tribute was demanded of these conquered lands, such as a certain number of bushels of wheat or
bales of wool or lumber or whatever products the land produced.
Finally David's kingdom reached from the Lebanon mountains

[1] The stories in this chapter are based on II Samuel 8; 9; 11; and 12; and 21:
1-15.

150

in the north to the desert of Arabia in the south, and from the Mediterranean Sea in the west to beyond the Jordan in the east.

The Luxury

As a result of all these conquests, King David grew rich. His court lived in luxury. The king also began to live at ease, leaving to his captains the actual hardships of war. David took more wives into his harem—often choosing prominent and beautiful women from the royal families of the defeated nations. More wives—and more children—required more royal houses, and even brought into the life of the court the worship of other gods than Yahweh.

In a few years' time, great changes took place in the daily habits of the people, not only in Jerusalem, but also in many other cities of the realm. Israel had become the one great nation on the eastern shores of the Mediterranean Sea. Their people traded with countries east and west, north and south. Certain families became wealthy, while the common people plodded away as farmers and hired laborers; and with each new conquest the number of slaves increased.

Unfortunately the more power David felt he had as king, the less sensitive he became to the feelings of others. He took advantage of the special privileges that people were accustomed to grant to kings. He did things that shocked and displeased even his best friends and advisers. At times he was extremely cruel in his treatment of his enemies.

Like other kings of the ancient world, David did not think it wrong to make his rule secure by getting rid of all rival claimants lest they plot to seize the throne. So he had all the seven descendants of Saul killed.

But when he realized that this might stir up the anger of the people of the north, he quickly tried to avert such a danger. He asked a former servant in King Saul's household one day: "Is there any one left of Saul's family to whom I may be kind for the sake of Jonathan?"

"There is Mephibosheth, a son of Jonathan, still alive," said the man, "but he is a cripple. He has been lame ever since he was a child and fell from his nurse's arms."

On learning of this young man, David immediately ordered

that Mephibosheth be brought to him. The king was extremely friendly, and as long as David lived this son of Jonathan lived in the palace and ate as one of the family at the king's table.

All for the Sake of a Woman

As the years passed, David spent more and more time in the safety of his own palace, where he lived at ease, surrounded by his pretty wives and his obedient servants in the luxury of a royal court.

One day while his faithful Joab and the armies of Israel were risking their lives in a war with the Ammonites, David arose from a late afternoon nap in his palace on the hill of Zion. He went up to the roof of his house and walked for a while. As he looked down upon the neighboring houses and grounds, he saw a woman bathing in a walled court nearby, and she was very beautiful to look upon.

At once David sent a servant to inquire who she was. Quickly the report came back: "Is it not Bathsheba, the wife of Uriah the Hittite? Her husband is now away with Joab in Ammon, fighting for the king."

Then David sent a messenger directly to Bathsheba and invited her to come at once to his palace. For several weeks after this David continued to invite her to visit him at the palace. Their friendship grew to passionate fondness, and David wanted her as his wife, even though he knew she was already the wife of Uriah, once of the bravest of his soldiers. Casting prudence aside, the king laid cruel plans to gain his end. He sent a message to Joab: "Send me Uriah the Hittite."

On Uriah's arrival, King David treated him with apparent friendliness. He asked questions about Joab and how the fighting was going. When Uriah finally returned home, the king sent with him a servant bearing a package of food from the royal table. But all the while, Uriah knew not of his wife's visits to the king.

When at last Uriah had to go back to his post, King David gave him a letter to take to his commander. Trustingly obedient, Uriah did not read the letter. Perhaps he could not have read it even if he had been bold enough to do so. He assumed it was as friendly as the king's conversations had been.

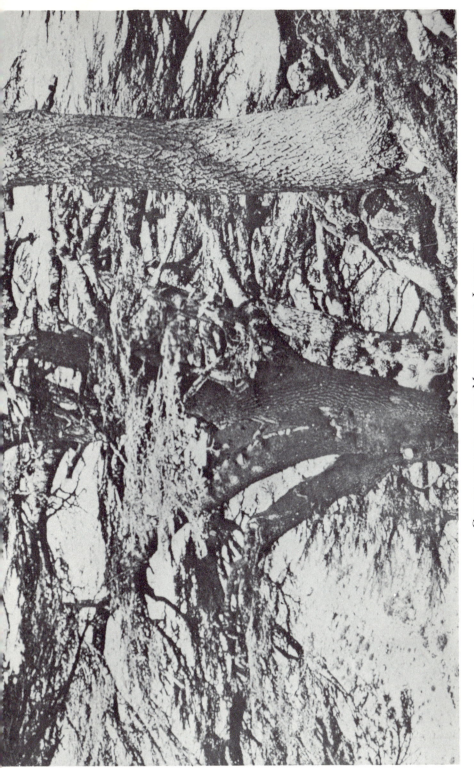

CEDARS ON ONE OF THE MOUNTAINS OF LEBANON

But when Uriah delivered the letter to Joab and the general opened the scroll to learn the message from the king, these were the words he read:

"Set Uriah in the front lines of the next battle in the hottest fighting so that he may be hit with an enemy arrow and die."

Not knowing at all why the king should give such instructions, Joab was astonished and grieved, for Uriah was a distinguished captain. Yet he was obedient to his king. When next he sent his men forth to attack the city, he placed Uriah in command of his most daring company and commanded him to lead in the attack.

Evidently in his zeal Uriah went with his men too close to the city wall. The attack was a complete failure. Some were hit by stones thrown from the top of the wall. Others were shot with arrows. And among the killed was Uriah himself.

As soon as possible, Joab sent a messenger back to Jerusalem to report the outcome of the battle and to give the names of the captains who were killed.

Joab expected David to be angry with his failure to capture the city. But instead, the king sent back this message to his commander:

"Let not this failure displease you, for the sword killeth one as well as another. Make your battle stronger next time against the city and conquer it."

When the wife of Uriah heard that her husband was dead, she mourned his loss. After a customary number of days for the mourning were past, David sent for Bathsheba and she became his wife. Later she became mother of a son for the king.

Nathan Boldly Accuses the King

Such a series of happenings awakened suspicious remarks in the king's household. Rumors of what had really happened became the subject of slanderous gossip. One of King David's old friends, Nathan the prophet, heard the shameful story. At first he could not believe that David could be guilty of such a disgraceful scheme. Nathan made sure of the truth before going to the king.

When Nathan finally stood in the king's presence, he began by telling him a story.

"There were two men in one city; the one was rich, and the

other was poor. The rich man had many large flocks of sheep and herds of cattle; but the poor man had nothing, except one lamb that he had owned ever since it was very little. This lamb had grown up in his household as if she were one of his children. The man had shared with her his own food. He had let her drink from his own cup and the lamb often lay with him on his bed and snuggled in his arms. The lamb was to the poor man as his own daughter.

"One day a traveler came to the rich man's house. The rich man wished to entertain him with a feast. But instead of killing and cooking one of his own many sheep to set before the weary, hungry traveler, the rich man sent a servant to take the poor man's only lamb, and commanded him to kill it and prepare it for the table. And so the rich man fed his guest."

Nathan paused here in his story, for he saw the king's face growing red and his eyes blazing with anger at the man who would do such a mean thing to a poor neighbor. David said to Nathan, "That man deserves to die and he should give four lambs to the poor neighbor on whom he had no pity."

Father and Child

This was just the effect which the prophet had wished his story to have. He looked calmly into David's eyes, and pointed his finger at the angry king and said in a low voice: "You are the man! You have been given the kingdom of Israel and Judah. You have riches and a great capital and a palace and many wives and children. Yet you killed Uriah. No—not with your own sword, but with the sword of a soldier of Ammon; and now you have taken Uriah's widow to be your wife!"

For a while David remained silent, unable to speak, for he suddenly saw the horrible point of Nathan's story as it applied to himself. Then he bowed his head in shame and confessed: "I have indeed committed a great sin. I deserve a terrible punishment from Yahweh."

Without further words, Nathan left David to think over his wrongdoing, and Nathan departed to his own house.

Shortly after this, Bathsheba's young baby was taken very sick. David prayed to Yahweh to spare the life of his child. He refused to eat and he lay all night upon the earth weeping and praying. He believed that the child's sickness was Yahweh's punishment for his great sin. The men of his household went to him and tried to raise him up from the earth. But he would not move, neither would he eat the bread they brought with them. Day after day passed. For a whole week David fasted and prayed and wept, until the seventh day when the child died. Then David arose, changed his clothes and went to the shrine of Yahweh and worshiped. When he returned to the palace, his servants set food before him, and he consented to eat.

The royal family were surprised at David's strange behavior, especially because he no longer wept after the child's death.

But David said, "While the child was still alive, I fasted and wept in the hope that Yahweh would be gracious to me and would permit the child to live. But now the child is dead. Why should I continue to fast and weep? Can I bring him back again? No! I shall go to him, but he will not return to me."

Later, when another son was born to Bathsheba, David felt that Yahweh's anger against him had finally passed. David named this new son Solomon—a name that means "Peaceable."

For a time King David was happy. His armies were on the whole successful in their wars against the neighboring states. All seemed to him to be going well with his growing kingdom.

19

Rival Claimants for the Throne

THE MAN WHO FOR MANY YEARS had been a fugitive wandering from cave to cave, in daily danger of a violent death, was now the great king of one of the most powerful nations of the ancient Near East. The man, once accustomed to the hardships of a hunter's life, one who was well able to face cold or heat, rain or winds, day and night in the open country, was now living in easy luxury with many beautiful wives to please him, and with kowtowing servants at his beck and call. The man once personally powerless, and in need of one friend at court, had now the power of life and death over many thousands of subjects. At his command armies of men had gone forth to fight the neighboring countries. At his command they brought tribute from these peoples to his capital. At his command thousands of workmen labored in mines and forests, fields and shops. They built for him palaces and storerooms and fortifications. It seemed as if the goal for the glory of Israel had at last been reached.[1]

In fact, for centuries after David, whenever the people of Israel grew discouraged over the sufferings and disappointments they sometimes had to bear, they hoped that "another David" or a descendant of the great king would come to save them and bring back again the glories of those early years.

But this is not the whole story of David. Darkening shadows, which threatened the happiness of the last days of this hero-king had been creeping into the scene.

As a warrior-king David had been successful, but as a father to his large family he was proving to be a sad failure. Perhaps he was so busy with affairs of state that he had little time left to give to his sons. The princes, enjoying all the luxuries of

---

[1] The stories in this chapter are based on II Samuel 13:1 through 19:8; I Kings 1: 5-53; 2: 1-12.

157

the royal court, and allowed to do almost anything they pleased, became selfish, disorderly, and unmanageable.

Jealousy Overcomes Absalom

David's second son, Absalom, was the king's favorite. In all Israel there was no one praised so much for his beauty as was Absalom. It was said that from the soles of his feet to the crown of his head there was nothing imperfect about his body. And as for his hair, it was extraordinarily heavy and beautiful, so that he took pride in wearing it long. But Absalom had more than beauty to commend him. He had a charming manner that made him popular with everyone who met him. He was King David's second son, however, and he was ambitious to become the king when his father died. Yet Absalom knew that this could never be brought about except by intrigue.

As he brooded over what he might do, he became more and more jealous of his older brother, Amnon, the heir apparent to the throne. Absalom for a while tried to be decent toward his brother, but as time passed, the fires of hate smoldered inside him, ready at any moment to burst into flame.

Now Amnon was a rather colorless person, and unaggressive; but he loved Tamar, his beautiful sister, with a deep affection. The handsome and charming Absalom began to tease Amnon by showing special attention to Tamar. But Absalom's affection was not true love. It was the feigned love of a jealous man who wanted to take revenge on his rival brother. The affair ended tragically two years later. Absalom did not kill Amnon himself, but he ordered his slaves to do so, at a time when Amnon was defenseless.

The whole royal household was so enraged that Absalom had to flee for his life and remain in exile for three whole years. David longed for the return of his much-loved son, but knew he must keep him in exile as a punishment and as a protection.

Joab, David's commander in chief, also liked Absalom and wished that he might be brought back home to be trained for his place as the eldest prince who would one day become king. Absalom, of course, was also anxious to return, for he still had ambitions to become king over Israel.

Many times Joab spoke to David, trying to gain the king's

favor toward Absalom, but without success. Joab persuaded
others to help him in this. He suggested ways in which they
might drop hints now and then to the king. Sometimes he even
told them exactly the words to say when they had opportunities
to speak with the king about his son Absalom.

Finally David was persuaded to let Absalom return from his
exile, but it was on condition that he would go directly to his own
house and live there quietly. David refused even to see his son.

The Rivals Become Stronger

For two years the king remained cold toward Absalom. This
seemed strange to those who knew how dearly the king had once
loved his son. What had happened? David was growing old, and
it would not be long before a choice of a successor would have
to be made. In court, jealousies and intrigues among the princes
increased, and the palace buzzed with rumors started by this or
that courtier who favored one or another of the king's sons.

The next oldest son was Adonijah. Some of the men of Israel
favored Adonijah. Others thought that the new king should be
elected by all the people, just as Saul and David had been. A
third group favored having the old king himself name his successor. More and more of the people at court favored this third
way. They were eager to know which son David himself wanted
to be his successor. They felt that someone was influencing him.
Who was it? And which of the sons was he favoring instead of
Absalom?

The answer soon became evident. Bathsheba had long been
David's favorite wife. She had a son named Solomon. Bathsheba
was ambitious that Solomon should become the next king.
There was even a rumor that the aging king had promised her
that her son should succeed him. Perhaps Bathsheba had been
responsible for David's refusal to forgive Absalom fully when he
returned home.

Absalom Courts Public Favor

As time went on, and Absalom still waited to be invited to
the palace, he grew impatient. He felt that he must do something to win his father's favor. Twice he asked Joab to arrange
for a meeting for him with his father; but nothing happened.

Absalom suspected that Joab was no longer his friend. In desperation he forced Joab to come to see him and made the commander take him to his father at the palace. The king welcomed his son with a kiss. It seemed that all was again friendly between David and Absalom.

Absalom, always popular among the young men, soon began to put himself forward to gain the attention of the people of Jerusalem. First he appeared in public in a fine chariot, driving two thoroughbred horses up and down the streets. Fifty footmen ran before him—as though he was practically king already.

He then tried to gain the affections of the people by sitting at the city gate, where all prominent visitors were bound to pass by, and where people from all over the country would come to seek justice for wrongs done to them. Whenever a man came and bowed down before him as a prince of the royal family, Absalom would quickly reach out his hand, draw the man to his feet, and greet him warmly, kissing him on the cheek as though he were an old friend. Then he would listen to the man's complaint and assure him that justice would be done. Absalom would say: "Yes, everything will be settled for you. I will see to that, for the king has appointed no one else to hear your plea." Then Absalom would shake his head sadly and murmur; but making sure that all would hear him: "Oh, that I were made judge in the land, that every man with a cause to plead might come to me, and I would give him justice!" So Absalom stole the hearts of the men of Israel.

Absalom's Open Rebellion

For four years Absalom kept himself in this way before the public at every opportunity. Finally, he felt that the time had come for him to take more direct action. He planned a rebellion to seize the throne. He thought that he had sufficiently won the favor of the people of Israel; now he must try to win the people of Judah. But he must not let anyone suspect his plans.

Absalom knew that Hebron had been his father's first capital, before he had brought the two kingdoms together into one. Absalom knew also that many people in Judah had resented David's establishing the capital elsewhere, even in Jerusalem. Absalom knew that in the south many had been growing more and more jealous of the increasing influence of the larger kingdom in the north. He would further stir their dissatisfaction against the aging David and win them over to support himself.

So Absalom went to the king and asked what seemed to be an innocent favor: "Let me go, I pray you, to Hebron where you, my father, were crowned king, for I made a vow, while I was in exile, that I would make a sacrifice to Yahweh at Hebron if ever I should be allowed to return there." Absalom managed his plan well, for his father did not suspect the scheme and allowed him to go.

In order to work more rapidly, Absalom took a large number of friends with him to Hebron to spread the word of his cause through the whole country. He sent secret messengers also into the north country, quietly saying to the people: "As soon as you hear the trumpets sound, you shall shout: 'Absalom is king in Hebron!'"

On the day determined by Absalom, men were stationed at many places throughout Judah and Israel, to blow the trumpets and rouse the people to shout the magic words proclaiming Absalom as king in Hebron. The revolt burst into flame everywhere. Only in Jerusalem could the rebellion be held down, because of the king's large gathering of troops in the capital. So quietly, yet steadily, had Absalom carried out his scheme that David had not heard of it before it was accomplished.

David Flees Weeping

When news of the rebellion reached the city, the weary and broken-hearted king decided to flee at once. He was not prepared to fight, and he feared for his own life and the lives of all his family. Quickly gathering together his wives and children, and all the courtiers and servants of the palace, he led them out through the east gate of the old city of which he had been so proud. Down into the Kidron valley they made their way. They were all barefoot and kept their heads covered, perhaps to disguise themselves. They waded the brook and climbed up the side of the Mount of Olives, weeping as they hurried along. Nor did they rest until they were safe on the other side of the Jordan.

Soon David discovered that one of his own trusted counselors,

Ahithophel, had aided Absalom in planning this rebellion. Ahithophel was the grandfather of Bathsheba, David's wife, and the king had thought this man would favor Solomon, his own grandson, for the kingship, as David himself had desired. But Ahithophel had never forgiven David for the treacherous way in which he had taken Bathsheba for his wife, and now Ahithophel was having his revenge by making trouble for David.

Perhaps it was this fact that made David decide not to give up the struggle at once, but to make an effort to recover his throne if possible. He secretly sent one of his servants, named Hushai, back into Jerusalem to act as a spy against Absalom and to keep him informed about everything the rebel king was planning to do.

A Wily Spy Gives Advice

Meanwhile Absalom occupied Jerusalem without a struggle, expecting to rule permanently as king in his father's place. He was trying to decide whether to pursue the fleeing king when the wily Hushai, pretending to be Absalom's friend, but really acting as David's spy, came to him exclaiming: "God save the king! God save the king!" And Absalom, knowing how friendly Hushai had been with David, asked: "Is this the way you show your loyalty to your old friend, David? Why did you not go with him?"

Hushai, still carrying out his pretense of friendliness toward Absalom, insisted: "On the contrary, whom Yahweh and this people have chosen as king, him will I serve and with him will I remain. Why should I not serve the king's son?"

"What do you advise me to do now?" asked Absalom. "Ahithophel thinks I should let him take a large force of men to pursue my father, the king, and take his life."

"Ahithophel's advice is not good," answered Hushai. "You know that your father has all his trained army of loyal soldiers with him. Now they are as angry as bears robbed of their young. They will fight more fiercely than ever. And even if you should succeed in defeating them, you would not find the king, for he would be hiding somewhere else."

Hushai was anxious to delay any action by Absalom against David, so that the fugitive king would have time to plan a

A Canaanite Nobleman on Parade

*When Absalom rode through Jerusalem with his footmen going before him,
he may have looked like this Canaanite ruler of Megiddo.*

campaign against his rebel son. Hushai continued: "I advise that
you begin gathering a great army of men from Israel and Judah,
for you have not enough now to make an attack. I believe, too,
that you, Absalom, should lead the army yourself. If you do
this, you will have a better chance to defeat your father's defenders and to capture him."

Strangely enough, Absalom followed Hushai's advice rather
than Ahithophel's. He could not bear the thought of making his
father the victim of such violence as Ahithophel wished, or of
putting him to death. So he set about collecting an army
throughout the kingdom.

Hushai lost no time in sending word to David of Absalom's
plans. This gave the old king time to prepare for the attack.
He gave orders at once to his skillful commander, Joab, to rally
his army and be ready to meet the rebels before Absalom could
form his army.

As Joab went out to the battle, David, still loving the son
who had proved so traitorous to his father, said to his commander: "Deal gently with the young man for my sake, if he
falls into your hands."

Before long, Absalom's hastily gathered, untrained troops
started eastward, expecting to make short work of David's defenders. But before the rebel army could take its position, Joab's
army had crossed the Jordan and met Absalom's forces somewhere on the fields of Ephraim. He gave the order for his men
to attack. Taken thus by surprise, Absalom's raw recruits, with

no commander as experienced as Jóab, took fright and began a confused retreat which ended in a rout.

Absalom himself, seeing the sudden turn of events, feared that he might be captured and treated only as a traitor should. He tried, therefore, to escape by riding his donkey into a patch of woods near-by. In his headlong rush, the young prince failed to dodge the low-hanging branches of the trees, and his head was caught by a forked bough of an oak, lifting him from his mount to hang, stunned and dying, while the beast galloped on.

When Joab was notified by one of his soldiers of the prince's fate, he ran quickly to the spot and found Absalom still barely alive. Without a moment's thought about David's command that he deal gently with the young man, Joab thrust three darts into the heart of Absalom, putting him to death. The rebel prince was buried in a pit in the forest where he met his death.

Victory Turns to Mourning

An African slave, a fast runner, carried the news, both of the victory and of Absalom's death. When the runner arrived at the king's house in Mahanaim, he cried: "News for my lord, the king! Yahweh has this day avenged you of all those who rose up against you."

David's first question was: "Is it well with the young man, Absalom?"

"May the enemies of my lord, the king, and all that rise up against you to harm you, be as that young man is," replied the slave.

At once David knew that Absalom was dead. Overcome with grief, he climbed the steps to an upper room to be alone with his sorrow. But as he went, those who stood near heard him sob: "O my son Absalom, my son, my son, Absalom! Would God that I had died for thee, O Absalom, my son, my son!"

The people of the city were at first relieved and happy to know that the king's army had been victorious. They were preparing to celebrate the triumph with wild rejoicing. But when the report went around that David was weeping for his son, all the people shared their king's grief, and their joy over the victory was suddenly turned to silent gloom. When the troops of the king, flushed with their victory, came back into the city expecting to be welcomed by cheering crowds, they were astonished to find only sad, mourning people everywhere. But the troops soon learned of their king's sorrow and joined in the silent grief of the city.

Not until Joab returned to his side did David rouse himself from his sorrow to speak to anyone. Joab, indeed, was vexed by the king's attitude and addressed him impatiently. "You are making all of us ashamed who have saved your life today," he said. "It seems almost as though you loved those who hate you and hate those who love you. The way you are acting, it appears that if Absalom had lived and all of us had died, you would have been pleased. You should go at once and thank those who took their lives in their hands to defend you against your traitorous son. You should be grateful for the brave men who died to save your throne. If you do not rise now and do this, you will have no one left to support you, for the soldiers will feel that they did wrong in defeating your enemies."

David saw the wisdom of doing as Joab advised, and the next day he sent a message to the people, expressing his gratitude to all who had been loyal to him. He went further and proclaimed pardon to all who had taken part in the rebellion against him.

All was peaceful again in Jerusalem, with the aged David back in his palace. But every one knew that the feeble king could not live much longer, and the question was being asked everywhere, "Who will become king after David?"

Adonijah Courts Public Favor

There were now just two rivals to the throne, Adonijah and Solomon, and it was believed that David himself favored Solomon, the son of his favorite wife, Bathsheba. On Adonijah's side were such important men as Joab and Abiathar. Favoring Solomon were Nathan, the prophet, and Zadok, the priest, and Benaiah, the captain of the king's bodyguard. And of course, Bathsheba was very ambitious to see her son Solomon on the throne.

Adonijah, knowing his father's preference for Solomon, began laying plans to seize the kingship in the same way that Absalom, his older brother, had tried to do. He made the same great show

of riding about with chariots and horsemen, and with fifty footmen running before him through the streets of Jerusalem. Then
he prepared a great feast to which he invited his brother princes
and many people from Judah. But he did not invite Nathan
or Benaiah or Solomon, or any of the supporters of his younger
brother.

Solomon Wins

Nathan immediately took action to defeat Adonijah's plans.
He went straight to Bathsheba and said: "Have you heard that
Adonijah is about to seize the throne, and David knows nothing
about it? Let me tell you what to do so that you may save your
life and that of Solomon, your son."

Nathan then outlined for Bathsheba a plan of action. "Go to
the king at once and say, 'Did you not make a promise to me, saying, "Surely Solomon my son shall reign after me and he shall
sit on my throne?" Why, then, does Adonijah now pretend to
be king?'

"While you are there speaking to the king," continued Nathan
to Bathsheba, "I will come in and confirm your words."

Bathsheba did as she was told, adding words of her own which
made it seem to the feeble king the most natural thing for him
to name his own successor, and not to place his eldest son on the
throne, nor yet allow the people to elect a new king. "See," she
said, "the eyes of all the people of Israel are upon you, expecting
that you will tell them who shall sit on the throne after you. If
you do not tell them now, then when you have died, the people
will think that I and my son Solomon have been rejected by
you."

Before she had finished speaking, Nathan was announced,
and David dismissed Bathsheba. The prophet bowed low and
said: "My lord, O king, have you proclaimed that Adonijah shall
reign in your place? He has made a great feast to which he has
invited the king's sons and the captains of the army and Abiathar
the priest. And they are all eating and drinking with him and
shouting, 'God save King Adonijah!' But he has invited neither
me, nor Zadok, nor Benaiah, nor Solomon. Is it possible that
this was arranged by my lord, the king, without telling us, your
advisers, who should sit on the throne after you?"

David quickly realized what was happening and without a moment's delay, he gave orders: "Call Zadok the priest, and Benaiah, the captain of my bodyguard."

When these men came before the king, David commanded "Go, order out my bodyguard. Set Solomon my son on my own mule and take him down to the fountain outside the city wall. There let Zadok and Nathan anoint him king over Israel. Then blow the trumpet and proclaim the word: 'God save King Solomon!' Then bring him here and he shall sit on the throne, for he shall become king in my place. I have appointed him this day to be king over Israel and Judah."

All was done as the king ordered. Crowds of people followed the company out of the city to the fountain, for they knew what it meant when they saw Solomon riding upon the king's own mule. When the anointing of Solomon had ended, the crowds followed the company back into the city, shouting: "God save King Solomon!" Soon the whole city rang with the cry.

All the while, in one of the king's houses on the hill, inside the city walls, Adonijah's guests were drinking to the health of their newly proclaimed king. Suddenly, the loud blasts of the priests' trumpets startled them. Then came the noise of the wild cheering and shouting as if from everywhere.

Presently a man ran into the room, crying, "Solomon has been crowned king—down by the spring—outside the city! David commanded it to be done." Adonijah and his guests were frightened. They rushed pell-mell from their tables and ran as fast as they could go, each to his own hiding place.

David lived but a short while after this exciting day, but he died peacefully, believing that Solomon would be king in his place and that there would be no more fighting between his sons for the crown.

20

Solomon's Dreams of Greatness

It was a pampered young prince of scarcely twenty years to whom David gave his crown. Born in a royal palace in the City of Jerusalem, after his father had made his major conquests, Solomon was a child of ease and comfort. So far as we know, he had never been called upon to test his physical courage in battle. The very name his father had given him meant "peaceable."[1]

Solomon's mother, Bathsheba, once the wife of a Hittite soldier, had become David's favorite wife. Her great beauty and charm cast a spell over the king and often influenced his actions. During his closing years she had won from him the choice of her son Solomon as successor to the throne. This was but the climax of a long series of special privileges that the young man had enjoyed from his babyhood.

Solomon was probably brilliant as well as charming. He must have had the most skilled scribes as his teachers. He early became interested in collecting proverbs found in the writings of the wise men of former times. It is also said that he took a special delight in riddles, just as màny another brilliant young man has done.

According to other legends told of Solomon, he must have enjoyed activities in the out-of-doors, since he became so famous later for his knowledge of nature. It was said that he could talk interestingly not only of the cedars of the forests but also of the delicate hyssop vine that grew in the cracks between the stones of the city walls. People were impressed by his knowledge of the flights of birds, of the ways of insects and fishes, as

---

[1] This chapter is based largely upon legends, the most famous of which is found in I Kings 3: 5-15.

well as of the habits of the wild animals of the woods. Solomon's knowledge of these things was probably of a practical sort rather than what today would be called scientific knowledge. He learned how to draw lessons from the ways of animals. Few scholars think he was the originator of all the proverbs which later generations have called the proverbs of Solomon. Yet it would not seem unreasonable to suppose that he was the author of some of them and the collector of many others.

Solomon took a great interest also in horses. He probably learned early how to drive in a chariot, and with this skill he could travel even beyond the boundaries of his land. An old legend is told of a visit he made as a prince to the king of Tyre. How his imagination must have been stirred by that amazing city by the sea, built upon the rocky heights of a small island! Perhaps it was in the king of Tyre's magnificent palace that Solomon first met the king's daughter and fell in love with her and secured the king's permission to take her as one of his queens. This same legend goes on to tell further of how the young Israelite prince went with the king of Tyre into his stately temple and joined in worshiping the god Baal-Melkart.[2]

Prince Solomon might also have visited the great dye factory on the mainland, not far from Tyre, where the flesh of thousands of shellfish, called the murex, was mashed in large vats in order to extract from it the purple dye for which the Phoenicians had become so famous.

One can imagine also that while the young prince was visiting in Tyre, he would walk down to the wharf and watch the sailors load their ships. He would ask what they were putting into the holds. Where were the ships bound? And when would they return? What lands and peoples would these sailors see? What riches would they bring back to their king? And so the young prince would learn of Egypt and Crete and Greece and Italy and Spain. Perhaps one day, as he looked from a window in the palace high up on the cliff above the harbor, Solomon may have watched one of these famous Phoenician fleets sail out to sea. And as he tried to imagine what might happen in the three long

---

[2] This legend is found in the writings of Clement of Alexandria, Strom. I, 114. Referred to by Dr. A. T. Olmstead in *History of Palestine and Syria* (New York and London: Charles Scribner's Sons, 1931), p. 340.

years those ships were to be gone, Solomon must have marveled at the skill and enterprise and courage that such adventures took.

Possibly Solomon was with the king of Tyre when one of these fleets returned, bringing home its precious cargoes. Then he would have heard the tales the sailors told of storms and tragedies, of beautiful lands and strange peoples. And did he see some of the treasures these voyagers brought back to their king? Painted vases, precious stones, beads, jewelry? Did he handle the pieces of copper and gold and silver that had been refined in the Phoenician refineries in Spain?

That the young Solomon actually saw for himself any of these foreign lands, of course, we can not be sure. But we do know that the young king was well aware of the wider world beyond his father's kingdom. The City of Jerusalem, in which Solomon lived throughout his childhood, was a place where foreigners were continually coming and going. The women in his father's harem had been brought from a number of different countries, and they must have talked with the royal children about the customs of these countries. Throughout his childhood, Solomon must have had many unusual opportunities to learn about the world of his day.

Out of all such experiences, he developed a large ambition. When he became king, he would surround himself with luxury and riches as the other kings of the nations. He would make the City of Jerusalem into one of the impressive capitals of the world. He would build a new and more magnificent palace than his father had built. And above his palace, on the top of the Hill of Zion, Solomon dreamed of a temple to Yahweh that would dazzle the world by its splendor.

He dreamed also of a royal court as lavish as that of the king of Tyre. When Solomon became king, he would not fight the kings of the nations around him. He would trade with them and so increase the riches of Israel. It was not large armies of soldiers that he would want. It would be armies of workmen he would need, men skilled as builders, carpenters, masons, stone-cutters, craftsmen in bronze and silver and gold and precious stones and ivory.

Thus the young Solomon dreamed of greatness. And he was bright enough to know that if he was to achieve these ends, he

himself would have to know more than his father, and he would
have to be wise in his making of plans. He would have to choose
his leaders carefully. He must be shrewd in his judgments of
men. He must organize his forces wisely. Yes, the young king
needed wisdom above everything else. If only he had wisdom,
then the power and glory of which he dreamed might be his too.

So King Solomon took his new responsibility as king very
seriously. His father had always consulted the God Yahweh
whenever he needed to make a difficult decision. King Solomon
decided to follow his father's way, but the son would make a
public occasion of his praying. And the ceremony would be held
on the hilltop outside the old city of Gibeon. On that ancient
altar the priest could make appropriate sacrifices, and any number of people could gather on the sloping hillside around it.

LUMBERMEN OF LEBANON
Cutting down cedar trees for an Egyptian Pharaoh.

Not long after the day of Solomon's crowning, a procession marched out through the northern gate of Jerusalem. At the head went the royal guards. Then came king Solomon and his counselors. These were followed by the white-robed priests and the musicians of the Jerusalem shrine. Some were playing harps and lyres, while still others were shaking tambourines or clanging their cymbals of brass. And last of all came the singing crowd of all kinds of people and officers of the Jerusalem tent shrine, who came prepared with the things needed for the great sacrifice. Some were leading large white oxen and sheep.

It was about a six-mile walk to Gibeon, over rocky paths and through the prickly brushwood in the forest. At last they could see the old walls of the town of Gibeon and the big stone altar high on the hill outside the town.

There hundreds of people from Gibeon and from the surrounding villages met them. While the crowd was gathering on the hilltop, they danced to the music of the harps and drums and sang old and familiar songs of Israel. Over and over again the shout would ring out: "Long live the king! Hail to Solomon the son of David!"

When at last the oxen and sheep had been slain and the smoke was curling upwards from the altar into the glowing sunset sky, King Solomon stood before the multitude and lifted his voice in a prayer of thanksgiving. In the presence of all these his people, he asked for wisdom that he might deal justly with them, and he promised before them all that he himself would obey Yahweh's commands and strive to do right. And he asked of Yahweh that the kingdom of Israel might prosper and that all might live in peace.

Late in the night when the feasting and dancing had ended, the people dispersed and returned to their homes rejoicing in their new king.

That night, as the story goes, King Solomon had a dream. In his dream, he saw the God Yahweh standing before him. God said, "Solomon, ask what you would most like to have me give you."

At once Solomon said, "O my God, you have shown great kindness to my father David. And now you have made me king instead of my father. But God, I feel like a little child who knows not how to carry out the difficult duties of a king. And yet I have been placed at the head of a very great people—more than I can number. Now, O God, I ask that you give your servant understanding so that he may see clearly what is right and what is wrong. Give me wisdom, O God, that I may give my people justice."

God was pleased with Solomon's prayer and said, "Because you have asked this thing and have not asked for riches, or for long life, or for fame, or for the lives of your enemies, but because you have asked for wisdom so that you may know justice. I shall grant your wish. You shall be wise, Solomon. But I shall give you riches also and a long life, and I shall make your kingdom so great that there shall not be another king as highly honored as you all your days. All this I promise you, provided you yourself do what is right and obey my commands."

When God had finished speaking, Solomon woke up and God had disappeared. Then Solomon knew that what had happened had been a dream. But he felt proud to think that his dream might come true.

Later he must have often told the dream to his courtiers and to his family. In those days men thought that such dreams were intended as promises that would come true.

And what a dream it was! In it were all the important things for which Solomon was ambitious—wisdom, long life, power, and glory! The dream itself faded away when Solomon awoke, but Solomon's ambitions guided his activities during all his reign of nearly forty years.

21

"Solomon in All His Glory"

His Ambitious Building Ventures

On his return to Jerusalem, King Solomon's plans quickly grew to vast proportions. He was planning at least six new buildings to stand on the slope leading up to the high plateau in the north-eastern part of the city. The plateau itself was the ancient site which David had purchased from Araunah for an altar.[1] On the lower and southern part of the slope was to be a grand assembly hall where public gatherings could be held. This large hall was to be supported by forty-five majestic pillars of cedar, each fifty feet high. These pillars were to be arranged in three long rows making a stately hall, one hundred and seventy feet long. The roof and the walls were also to be made of cedar beams.[2]

One day when King Solomon was talking over his plans, Azariah, the architect, said laughingly, "We shall have to call this the House of the Forest of Lebanon for the many pillars will make it look like a forest."

"A fitting name!" said Solomon. "That is what it shall be called."

Above this assembly hall, King Solomon planned an open porch, also marked off with tall cedar pillars. And this porch was to be the entrance into the King's own judgment hall beyond. At one end of this hall was to stand the throne. Six steps were to lead up to the royal chair. Beside each arm of the chair was to stand a golden lion, and on the two ends of each step were to stand other golden lions. The whole throne was to be made of sandalwood and decorated with designs in ivory and the wood was to be overlaid with gold. Yes, King Solomon would

---

[1] II Samuel 24: 18-25.

[2] The stories in this chapter are based on I Kings 3: 16-28; 4: 26; and chapters 5 through 10. Findings from archaeological explorations and comparative history are also used.

174

spare no money to make the royal throne, if possible, even more elaborate than that of the king of Tyre.

And higher up the slope above the throne room was to stand the largest and most costly of the buildings—King Solomon's own palace and courtyard. Attached to its northwest corner was to be the palace of King Solomon's Egyptian wife.

On the plateau which crowned the slope was to be built the great temple to the God Yahweh. This would not be the biggest building on the hill, but it would be the most conspicuous and the most exquisitely ornamented. This temple was not to be a place of public worship in which great crowds would gather, but a royal sanctuary in which worship *for* the people rather than worship *by* the people could be held.

Finally, when all these buildings had been completed, a great stone wall was to be built enclosing all the buildings on the hill.

Such ambitious plans would require great sums of money and large numbers of workmen. The people of Israel had not yet learned the skills needed to build such buildings. Nor were the Israelites accustomed to being summoned to such labor by their king. The number of paid laborers that King David had secured was small compared with the large number King Solomon would need.

It is natural, then, that the young king should first turn for help to Hiram, the king of Tyre.[3] Soon a message was on its way to Phoenicia. In it King Solomon hinted at some of his building plans:

"I intend to build a palace and a hall of judgment and a temple in my royal city. And I shall need for these buildings many pillars of cedar fifty feet in length. You know, my friend, that there is none among us who knows how to cut down such trees. Your men are skilled. I ask you, therefore, to command your men to cut down cedar trees and to bring them to us. I ask you also that some of my workmen be allowed to work with yours so they may learn the skills that they now lack. I assure you, O king, that I will give you the wages required for your men, whatever amount you may ask."

The king of Tyre was pleased to receive this request from

---

[3] The king of Tyre at this time was Hiram. He is inaccurately presented in the Biblical account as ruling during the early years of David's reign.

King Solomon, and wrote back, "I have the message which you sent me. I shall be glad to do all that you ask. I shall send you cedar logs and also fir trees if you need them. My workmen will bring these logs down from the forests of Lebanon to the seashore. There they will make them into rafts to be floated to whatever port you may name. From there the logs can be carried on wheels and pulled along the roadways to your city. For all these services you may pay me back in food. You have many farmers in your country and we need the wheat and wine and olive oil that they produce."

So the agreement was made between the two kings.

King Solomon appointed Adoniram to be the chief in charge of gathering the vast numbers of workmen needed. He appointed an enterprising young northerner named Jeroboam as Adoniram's chief assistant in this enormous task. These men were to go or send their representatives to all parts of the country. These officers drafted hundreds of men—both free Israelites and slaves —and organized them into working gangs. For one month they were to be required to work for the king wherever he might send them. Then for two months they might return to their masters and work for them. Naturally such measures did not please the farmers. Neither were the men themselves always happy about leaving their families to work at these new tasks for which they had not been trained. But there was no chance to appeal. The king was king and his orders had to be obeyed. It is reported that it took seven years to build the temple in Jerusalem and that it took thirteen years to build his palace.

The Temple Is Dedicated

To most of the people of Israel, the greatest of all these under-takings was the building of the temple; and the day of its dedication was unforgettable. People from every part of the country gathered in the capital city. Representatives were there from all the twelve divisions of the kingdom. All the head men from the towns of Ephraim and Judah who could possibly come were surely there—and all the princes of the royal house and all the priests who were to conduct the temple services. Thousands came. Every house in the city was crowded with guests. Tents were set up on the hills outside the city walls to the north.

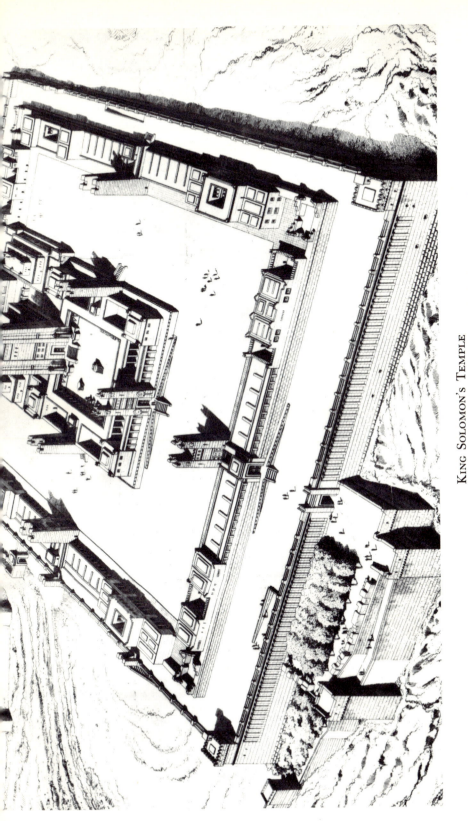

KING SOLOMON'S TEMPLE

A drawing by C. H. Chipiez, who used the ideal temple described in Ezekiel, chapter 40, for his source.

It was in the lovely harvest time of the year, and the people had brought gifts from their fields. It was to be a week of excitement, of feasting and dancing and singing and of stately ceremonies.

Early the first great morning, even before sunrise, the procession began to form in the streets of the lower city. Through the great gate in the southern and lower wall of the great enclosure on the slope leading up toward the temple they passed. First came the royal bodyguard, then a band of musicians playing upon harps and timbrels and clanging cymbals, while others behind danced and sang. Then came four white-robed priests. The sacred ark rested on poles laid upon their shoulders.

Behind the ark came King Solomon, robed in all his glory, followed by more priests and the king's many counselors. Then came the queens and princes and princesses and attendants of the royal court. And last of all followed more musicians and white-robed singers and a motley crowd of men, women, and children from all parts of the land. All those to whom the temple was a place of wonder were there to participate in the ceremonies of this great day.

Past the great Hall of the Forest of Lebanon they came, and up by the open, pillared porch, and then along the eastern entrance to the royal hall of judgment. Most of the people had not yet seen inside that stately hall, where stood the king's great throne of gold and the twelve golden lions standing on either side of the steps leading up to the royal chair. But those who had seen the throne had spread glowing reports of its magnificence. Then the procession wound its way around the palaces and on up to the eastern gate in the wall surrounding the great temple enclosure.

And there they stopped. The great iron gates were closed.

The men carrying the sacred ark paused before the bottom steps. Then the choir began singing as the harps played and the timbrels were thrummed:

> Lift up your heads, O ye gates,
> And be ye lifted up, ye everlasting doors,
> That the King of Glory may come in!

A chorus from behind the doors chanted a response:

> Who is this King of Glory?

The singers outside sang back:

> Yahweh, strong and mighty,
> Yahweh, mighty in battle!
> Lift up your heads, O ye gates,
> Yea, lift them up, ye everlasting doors,
> That the King of Glory may come in!

Then the great iron doors swung slowly open and the four men carrying the ark walked up the steps and into the great wide court, and on toward the next open door of the temple itself where they waited once more for their time to enter.

The great crowd slowly gathered behind them. And there they waited, awed by the height and splendor of the temple walls rising before them. Above the crowd hung the spacious blue dome of the sky and over the eastern wall of the court the rising sun seemed to beam a blessing down upon them.

Directly before them to the west stood the temple, set on a platform ten steps above the court. The great cedar doors were open, and the morning sunshine was pouring in. Those who were close enough could see the light stream clear across the full length of the next court. It seemed as though its beams pointed to the very doorway of the Holy of Holies, where the sacred ark was soon to stand.

Most of the people in the large outer court were not allowed to go farther into the sacred temple. But there was enough for them to see right there to cast a spell of awe upon them. Before them, the massive stone walls surrounding the inner court rose high above their heads; and beyond and above these walls gleamed the towers of the royal sanctuary. And right before their eyes, and only a few feet in front and on either side of the great cedar doors, stood the two majestic bronze pillars that everyone had been talking about. Higher than the cedar doors, higher than the walls of the next court, these two pillars stood like giant watchmen before the House of Yahweh.

Those of the crowd who were permitted to go up into the inner court could see the great stone altar in the center and the priests waiting in line to perform the sacrifices. Only a few of the crowd were able even to catch a glimpse through the next doors beyond that led into the main hall of the royal sanctuary itself. As onlookers, they formed in ordered ranks to watch the ceremony. Again the singing began, and the priests carried the ark, followed by the king and his attendants, up the steps and through the wide doors of the royal shrine. Slowly the bearers of the ark carried their precious burden down the length of the great room to the doorway of the innermost shrine, the Holy of Holies.

Finally, while choirs sang and harpists played, the ark was borne in through the door and set down between the great over-arching wings of two golden cherubim. There the sacred box was to remain permanently in the darkness. It was to be a perpetual symbol to the people of Israel that Yahweh, their God, was with them.

Then, when the ark had been safely put in its sacred place and the door had been closed, King Solomon, so glorious in his purple robes, walked back to the open door of the temple and stood between the two bronze pillars. The sunlight fell directly on him, and the purple and gold of his royal robes shown with a dazzling beauty.

A hush came over the people while King Solomon spoke,

> Yahweh has set the sun in the heavens,
> But he said that he would dwell in darkness.
> I have built thee a house for thy dwelling place,
> A place where thy presence will abide for all time.[4]

Then he lifted up his face toward the sky and prayed,

> O Yahweh our God, listen to the prayer of thy servant, and to all the prayers of thy people Israel, when they shall pray toward this place. Yes, hear them from thy dwelling place, and when thou hearest, forgive.[5]

After this ceremony, the flesh of many animals was burnt upon the great altar in the temple court. The celebrations continued morning after morning for several days. When the people at last pulled up the stakes of their tents and said good-by to their hosts in Jerusalem, they returned to their homes feeling strong and happy. They said, "Yahweh our God has been good to us," and, "Long live Solomon our king!"

---

[4] I Kings 8: 12, 13. This is quoted from the Septuagint.
[5] I Kings 8: 30. This is part of a long prayer of dedication composed apparently by later writers, but this sentence seems most appropriate to the occasion.

For King Solomon, the dreams of his youth had come true. Israel was now a great nation, and the capital City of Jerusalem was famous throughout his known world.

His Trade by Land and Sea

During these years of activity in building up Jerusalem, and for some years afterwards, King Solomon had many workmen busy in many other parts of his kingdom, constructing defenses and buildings of many kinds. Ruins of such projects have been found in widely scattered cities from the north to the south ot the land of Palestine.

All these enterprises of King Solomon required continued drafting of men and provisions from his kingdom, as well as the finding of new ways to pay for his vast undertakings. But King Solomon's ability to plan was equal to his need.

He soon succeeded in establishing a wide trade in horses and chariots. Before this, chariots had been used either for pleasure or by armies. But now Solomon increased the demand and the supply by buying and selling both horses and chariots, building up a large market for them and thus greatly adding to his profits. He bought horses from Cilicia (in southern Asia Minor) and chariots from Egypt, and sold them to kings of the Hittites and of Syria. This growing trade required the building of large stables in a number of different cities in his realm. Archaeologists have found in Megiddo on the Plain of Esdraelon the ruins of one of King Solomon's stables where at least four hundred horses and chariots could have been housed. Eventually King Solomon built up such a trade that the number of horses and chariots he owned ran into the thousands.

In addition to all these undertakings, King Solomon must have had representatives covering a number of different countries. These men were continually on the lookout for other ways of gaining riches. Some of King Solomon's scouts were in Edom, a land that King David had subdued, which lay south of the Dead Sea. These Edomites brought regular tribute to Israel.

But Solomon coveted more of the iron and copper that was to be had from the mines of Edom. He was ambitious to extend his trade to other countries to the south, along the shores of the Red Sea and down the coast of Africa to the lands of Punt and

Ophir. At the southern tip of Edom and on the north end of the Red Sea was the little town of Ezion-Geber—lying like an open doorway to this whole region. If the kings of Tyre had enriched their land by extending their trade far across the Mediterranean Sea, why could not King Solomon do the same on the Red Sea?

There were at least three reasons why not, and most monarchs would have regarded them as serious. The Israelites had no harbor in the Red Sea and no ships; and also the crude iron and copper ores that came from the mines of Edom were too bulky to ship to distant places. King Hiram of Tyre had his own smelting plants and factories even as far off as Spain and the island of Sardinia. But Israel probably had no smelting plant of any size and few men who knew the art of smelting.

So King Solomon's first big undertaking was to build a good harbor beside the town of Ezion-Geber, where ocean-going sailing vessels could load and unload. He also began building, just north of the harbor, a smelting plant where the iron and copper ores from Edom could be refined, and a factory where his men could make, out of these metals, articles that could be sold.

Who but King Solomon would have dared such a venture? And in such a disagreeably hot place as Ezion-Geber where the winds continually blow the sand into one's face! But it was just these winds that led King Solomon's counsellors to decide upon this place, for the winds could always be counted on. The furnaces were built with holes in just the right places so that they would catch the winds, and the winds would keep the fires burning. Dr. Nelson Glueck, who has dug into the ruins of this refinery and factory, has expressed his amazement at this record of King Solomon's "wealth, power, wisdom and energy."[6] For the building of this smelting plant and factory, hundreds of workmen must have been gathered from the families of Israel and Edom, and brought all the way down to this southern port and taught how to do this difficult work. In addition all these men had to be housed, fed, and paid!

---

[6] Nelson Glueck, *The Other Side of the Jordan* (New Haven, Conn.: American Schools of Oriental Research, 1940); also *Bulletin of the American Schools of Oriental Research*, No. 75, October, 1939), pp. 10, 12, 17, 20.

But why refine the iron and copper in this harbor if Solomon had no ships to carry these products to other lands? So the next step in the king's ambitious plans was to build ships of his own so that he could send to these far-off lands to the south and east. Again King Solomon turned to King Hiram, for there were no shipbuilders in Israel. And on the first voyage would King Hiram be good enough to let a crew of his skilled navigators go along with Solomon's inexperienced seamen so that they might learn the art of sailing? Again King Hiram agreed to King Solomon's proposal.

Although it must have taken years to work out these tremendous plans, there finally came a day when King Solomon's own ships sailed out of the harbor of Ezion-Geber, bound for the lands of Punt and Ophir. Perhaps two or more years later, these same seamen sailed back into port to tell their tales of adventure. And in their ships they carried rich cargoes of elephants' ivory tusks, much sandalwood, silver and gold, many precious stones, and even little monkeys.

With all these developments of trade and commerce, King Solomon greatly increased the wealth and prestige of his kingdom as well as his own reputation as a wise and energetic and powerful ruler.

The Visit of the Queen of Sheba

The extent to which other people were being impressed by the extraordinary growth of this powerful nation is shown by the legend that is told of the queen of Sheba. Her people were Arabians who lived on the southern shore of the Arabian peninsula. Before King Solomon's ships came sailing down the Red Sea and on out to the Indian Ocean, the kingdom of Sheba was doing a thriving trade around the Red Sea. But now things were changing. King Solomon's ships were passing it by and gathering most of their treasures from the land of Ophir.

The queen of Sheba proposed to her counselors that she go herself as an ambassador to King Solomon and make a treaty with him, so that her country might get some of his trade. It was a daring adventure. Would this young monarch receive her at all? Might he compel her to join his harem? Or might he even have her imprisoned?

The queen of Sheba was not only beautiful. She was clever too. She would awaken King Solomon's interest in her people by bringing him lavish gifts, samples of their most exquisite workmanship. And she would speak to him with modesty and flatter him with words of praise. She had heard amazing tales of his wisdom and his ability to answer riddles. She would pretend to test his wisdom, and she would be astonished at his answers.

So the queen of Sheba came to Jerusalem with a very long caravan of camels, bearing gifts of spices and very much gold and silver and precious stones.

When she was presented before the throne, she spoke with the most flattering praise of the wonderful things she was seeing and of the tales she had heard of King Solomon's wisdom. She asked him many questions, and Solomon never failed to answer them. The queen of Sheba found out for herself how wise the king was. She was shown all the great buildings. She ate in his palace and noted the sumptuous amounts of food served at the royal table. She watched the way each courtier did his part, and she saw how happily the many servants waited on their king. She visited the temple and watched the priests make the sacrifice of oxen on the great altar. When the queen had seen all these things, she had no more pride left in herself and in her little country.

She said, "It was a true report, O king, that I heard in my own land of your great activities and of your wisdom. But I could not believe those reports until I came and my own eyes have seen. Indeed the half was never told me."

What monarch could resist such praise from a beautiful queen! It is easy to imagine how after this a plan was happily worked out between the king and queen whereby the people of Sheba from that time on shared in the trading carried on by King Solomon's fleet.

The Tale of the Two Mothers

Many legends have been handed down reporting the great wisdom of Solomon, but no other is quite so universally famous as the story of the two mothers.

Two women stood before King Solomon's throne. One was

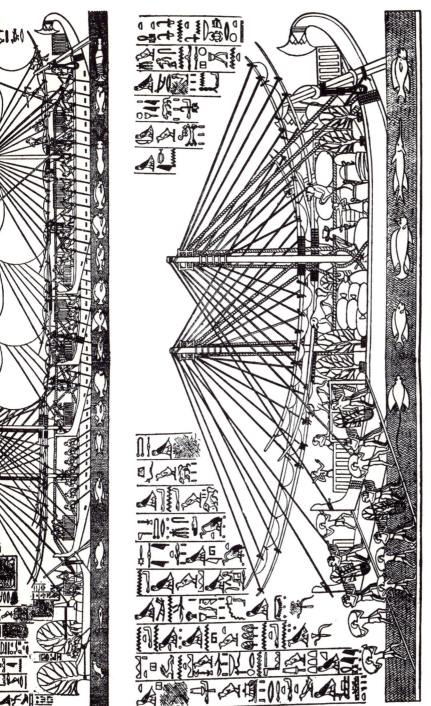

A MERCHANT FLEET

King Solomon's fleet was probably much like this fleet of Queen Hatshepsut of Egypt. This painting was found on the wall of her temple at Deir el-Behri near Thebes. The upper part shows the fleet starting out for the Land of Punt. The lower part shows a ship being loaded for the return trip. Note the men carrying myrrh trees on board; the monkeys, the bags, the jars of precious things; and the officers giving orders.

carrying a small baby. The other woman who came without a child spoke first.

"Oh gracious and wise king! This woman and I both live together in the same house. A baby was born to me, and three days later she too had a baby. We were alone in the house. No one else was with us. Our babies were both boys and looked much alike. Then one night while both of us were asleep, this woman's baby died.

"When she awoke and discovered that her baby was dead, she was horrified because she had unknowingly lain on the child and smothered it. She did not wake me or call to me for comfort. Instead, she rose quietly from her bed at midnight and picked my baby from beside me while I slept and laid it in her own bed. Then she picked up her own dead baby and brought it to lie beside me.

"When I awoke in the morning to give my child a feeding, behold, I found that the baby beside me was dead. Since the night was then far gone and light shone in through the window, I looked more carefully at the baby's face. Then I realized that it was not my boy at all.

"I went over to this woman's bed where she was holding a live baby in her arms. I looked into his face and I recognized it was my own child. I said so to her and asked her what had happened. She pretended that nothing had happened. She said, 'This living baby is mine. The dead one is yours.'

"And I said, 'No, the living baby is mine and the dead one is yours.' In this way, O king, we have been disputing ever since."

When the woman had finished her story, the other woman with the baby in her arms began at once to contradict her. "The living baby *is* mine," she said, "and the dead baby is hers."

Finally, King Solomon called an attendant. "Fetch me a sword," he said. When the sword was brought to the king, he took it in his hand, and watched the faces of the two women intently as he spoke. "Cut this living child in two and give one half to one of these women and one half to the other." The shocked servant took the sword from the king and started to take the child from the woman's arms.

But the other woman screamed, "O my Lord, give her the living child. By no means kill it."

But the other said, "Let it be as the king commands. The child shall be neither yours nor mine."

Then the king knew. He said, "Give the living child to the mother who really wants it. She is the true mother."

Whenever this story was told in a market place or around a family table, someone always shook his head and said, "King Solomon is very wise. He knows how to decide when justice is at stake."

But the wisdom of Solomon as well as his riches have been greatly exaggerated.

The stories of King Solomon's wisdom grew with the telling. The queen of Sheba paid him a flattering visit. Later it was said: "All the kings of the earth came to hear of his wisdom." Because he collected many proverbs from the writings of wise men of the past, it was said later that King Solomon himself thought up three thousand proverbs and that these are the ones found in a book of that name that is part of the Bible.

Because King Solomon carried on such large trading ventures, it was said that Solomon exceeded all the kings of the earth in riches and wisdom.

> And all the kings of the earth . . . brought every man his tribute, vessels of silver and vessels of gold, and raiment, armor and spices, horses and mules, a rate year by year. And Solomon had four thousand stalls for his horses and chariots and twelve thousand horsemen . . . And the king made silver to be in Jerusalem as stones, and cedars made he to be as the sycamore trees that are in the lowland in abundance.[7]

[7] II Chronicles 9: 23-25, 27.

22

The Northern Masses Rebel

THE GLORY OF SOLOMON became the glory of extravagance. He was ambitious to make his own name great upon the earth. The development of his fantastic trade with foreign countries was not intended to make the majority of his people happier and their living conditions healthier. King Solomon did not search for beauty for all to enjoy. He only wanted his cities, his buildings, his court, to be more luxurious than those of any other king. His friendliness with foreign nations was not inspired by a desire for mutual sharing. He made friends in order to exploit other peoples for his own gain. King Solomon's harem of hundreds of wives, a much larger number than David had had, was not for love but for show. Many of these wives were daughters of foreign rulers and were taken by Solomon in order to make more binding the treaties he had made with those rulers, and thus to insure peace and profitable trade with their countries.

The thousands of workmen whom he took away from the farmers and whom he forced to labor away from their homes and children—how could they think well of him?

The men who had to toil in those hot and sand-blown regions of Edom, working over the furnaces where iron and copper were melted to white heat—how could they be happy?

The farmers and landowners who had to hand over to their king larger and larger amounts in taxes—how could they be enthusiastic over these wonderful buildings?

But men and women, once under the power of a dictator, have a difficult time freeing themselves.

King Solomon was doubtless unaware of his selfishness. He was doing as all the great kings of whom he knew had done. The only difference between them and him was that he was more successful than most. Solomon reigned in Jerusalem nearly forty years. It was probably not until near the end of his life that he realized there was a group of discontents who were secretly talking of rebellion.

His building enterprises never seemed to end. All the six great buildings that he had dreamed of were now completed in Jerusalem. The walls surrounding the entire area had all been built. But King Solomon had another dream. There were two hills on which the ancient City of Jerusalem stood, the Hill of Zion (David's city) and the Hill of Moriah to the north, on which Solomon built the temple. Between these hills was a small ravine. King Solomon had never forgotten what King Hiram had accomplished—how he had joined that small rocky island of Tyre to the mainland by building a bridge of stones and clay mud across the channel between them. King Solomon surely could build a bridge of earth between the two hills of the city of Jerusalem. How big a help such a bridge would be to everyone who wanted to go from one hill to the other! And how impressive such a roadway would be!

Now for many years King Solomon had been hearing about Jeroboam, that capable assistant of Adoniram's who seemed able to get more work out of his men than any other overseer. Surely Jeroboam would be just the man to supervise the workmen on this new undertaking.

But during the many years that Jeroboam had been supervising these hundreds of workmen, he had been hearing their complaints. Secretly he had long been sympathizing with them, but he had not dared to let them know. Finally his own sense of justice had forced him to take their side. This was quite natural, since he himself was a northerner and had been brought up as a farmer. It had been most distasteful to him to pull these workmen off the northern farms and to force them to work in Jerusalem or at Ezion-Geber or elsewhere in the country at tasks in which they had no interest.

Jeroboam accepted the job that King Solomon offered him, but he used it as an opportunity to start a secret rebellion. "Let the people of Judah have their own kingdom," he said. "Let them build these great cities and carry on this world-wide trade, but let us in the north separate from them and keep our own kingdom. Let us live quietly under our own vines and fig trees. Let us worship our god in the simple shrines we have in all our towns. Why go up to Jerusalem? Why pay these large taxes? Let us be free!"

Rumor of this smoldering rebellion at last reached the ears of King Solomon. He quickly sent his officers to search for Jeroboam with orders to kill. But Jeroboam fled to Egypt, where he remained in hiding. He knew he would not have long to wait, for King Solomon was an old man by this time, having reigned nearly forty years.

Finally the word was passed around: "King Solomon is dead!" A friend of Jeroboam swiftly carried the word to him in Egypt. In Jerusalem, the people took the news of their king's death without alarm. There was no question in the minds of most of the people who would be the new king. Rehoboam, the oldest son, of course, was the rightful heir. He was promptly crowned by the chief priest, with the usual ceremonies, and the usual shouting and feasting were added.

But Rehoboam was not ignorant of the rebellion that had been started in the north. Few northerners had been in Jerusalem for the royal ceremonies. Just to be on the safe side, therefore, he decided it would be wise to go to some town in the north and have another public celebration there. He chose Shechem for this. Of course, he expected that the ceremonies would all be a mere formality, but it was important that the northern tribes be given an opportunity to see that he had now become the king of all Israel—both north and south.

Crowds gathered as they had for his father. There was dancing and singing and the playing on harps and the beating of drums and the clanging of cymbals and the shouting of "God save King Rehoboam!" But not everyone joined in the festivities. Some stood back watching. There seemed to be less enthusiasm than Rehoboam had expected. What was the matter?

Then there was a surprise. In the midst of the noise and shouting a small band led by none other than Jeroboam came into the crowd! The northerners were both glad and frightened. The rebel was back. What would happen? Some expected Rehoboam to order him seized at once.

But Jeroboam and his followers stepped boldly forward. They bowed before Rehoboam. Then Jeroboam spoke for them all.

"Your father made our burdens heavy and grievous. If you

THE GREAT ALTAR FOR BURNT OFFERINGS IN THE TEMPLE COURT

To the left, on twelve bronze oxen, rests the bronze laver for the water needed in the sacrifices.

will lighten our burdens and make them less grievous we will serve you as our king."

Rehoboam had not expected such a straightforward request. He was puzzled to know how to answer. He waited. Finally he said: "Go back home for three days. Give me time to think over my plans. Then come back to this place and I will answer you."

The people departed. Rehoboam first asked the advice of the old men who had always guided his father in his decisions. "What answer shall I give to these people?"

"Tell these people that as a king your interest will be to serve them and that you will be kind to them. Speak favorably to them so that they are not afraid of you. Then they will be loyal to you forever."

Rehoboam then went to the young men who had grown up with him in Jerusalem and who would soon be among his counselors. "What answer shall I give?" he asked; and the young men said, "Tell the people that your little finger is thicker than your father's thigh. If he made their work heavy, you will make it even heavier. If he whipped them with whips, you will whip them with stinging scorpions."

Three days later the people gathered at the shrine outside the walled town of Shechem. A large number of armed soldiers surrounded Rehoboam on either side as he stood before them at the top of the hill. His voice was harsh and his eyes were arrogant as he addressed them.

"My father made your burdens heavy. I will add to your labors. My father whipped you with whips. I will whip you with stinging scorpions." [1]

When the people heard these words, they cried out angrily: "What part have we in the dynasty of David! Ye people of Judah, go back to your houses! We of the north will see to our own affairs!"

Rehoboam's bodyguards, seeing the danger the king was in, quickly hurried him off to his chariot. And he and they fled as fast as they could back to Jerusalem. There Rehoboam con-

---

[1] "Scorpion" appears to be the name given to a leather-covered club, like a blackjack with metal points, used to beat prisoners or to drive workmen or slaves.

tinued to rule the people of the south. But when he sent Adoniram out to force the labor gangs to work for the king, the men
threw stones at him till he died.

In the north, the people rallied around Jeroboam and made
him their king. So it was that the powerful nation that Solomon
thought he had built broke into two small kingdoms. The city
of Samaria in the north became a rival capital to the city of
Jerusalem. The large trading projects that King Solomon had
developed began to decline. Fewer people came to the temple
in Jerusalem to worship. The glory and riches and fame of the
empire of Solomon began to shrivel and decay.

Each of these two kingdoms was made weaker by the division, and in a few centuries both were completely destroyed by
neighboring nations who in turn seized their opportunities for
conquest. Thousands of the people of Israel and Judah became
captives in foreign lands. The northern kingdom of Israel disappeared altogether, never to recover. The southern kingdom
of Judah was later partly restored when a few thousand of the
refugees were permitted to return. The temple was rebuilt, but
again destroyed, then again rebuilt. But all the while, except for
a few short years, the people of Israel were ruled by foreign
kings. The third temple in Jerusalem was destroyed by the
Romans in the first century A.C.E.

Ever since then the people of Israel, now called the Jews, have
been scattered. They have migrated into every continent. Some
can probably be found in every country of the world. And until
the twentieth century no effort to bring even a few of them together into one nation has been successful.

As we try to look back over these centuries of struggle and
war, we are impressed by the fact that the famous men in this
drama of ancient Israel were military leaders and rulers. However much they accomplished in conquering the land and in
establishing a monarchy, they were impelled largely by ambitions to rival and surpass the other nations of their times. They
built up what they thought would be a strong and enduring
nation, but it was at the expense of other peoples and even of
the highest welfare of their own nation. Solomon especially,
coveting power and magnificence above all else, brought about
a way of life which gave luxury and ease to the few but doomed

the many to hardship, want, and suffering. He failed to realize
that

> We all are blind until we see
>   That in the human plan
> Nothing is worth the making if
>   It does not make the man.
> Why build these cities glorious
>   If man unbuilded goes?
> In vain we build the world, unless
>   The builder also grows.[2]

The greater men of Israel have been the sturdy, daring souls
called the prophets, who lived a century and more after the
division of the kingdom. They protested against the very evils
that had their beginnings during the dramatic period we have
just described. These prophets, often at the risk of their lives,
spoke boldly against the wrongs and the oppressions suffered by
their people at the hands of shortsighted and arrogant leaders.
They sounded a stirring call for justice among men and for
sincerity in religion. But the story of these prophets must be
reserved for another book.

---

[2] Edwin Markham, "Man-Making," in *Gates of Paradise and Other Poems*" (New
York: Doubleday, Page and Company, 1920), p. 20. Copyright 1920 by Edwin
Markham. Reprinted by permission of Virgil Markham.

Dates for the Events Described

Reign of Akhenaten of Egypt .... c. 1377 - 1360 B.C.E.

Destruction of Jericho .... c. 1377 - 1300 B.C.E.

Exodus of Israelites from Egypt .... c. 1290 B.C.E.

Entrance of Joshua into Canaan with Israelites
from Egypt .... c. 1250 - 1200 B.C.E.

Victory of Gideon and Deborah .... c. 1150 B.C.E.

Reign of Saul .... c. 1020 - 1004 B.C.E.

Reign of David .... c. 1004 - 960 B.C.E.

Reign of Solomon .... c. 960 - 925 B.C.E.

Division of the Kingdom .... c. 925 B.C.E.

B.C.E. means "Before the Common Era." In Christian tradition, the usual letters used are "B.C.," meaning "Before Christ." We prefer the form on which both Christians and Jews can unite.

The letter "c." stands for the latin word "*circa*," meaning "around" or "about."

Table of Pronunciations

MEANINGS OF MARKS

ā	as in *mate*	e	as in *get*	o	as in *not*
ä	as in *father*	ī	as in *mine*	oo	as in *food*
a	as in *hat*	i	as in *pin*	ū	as in *use*
ē	as in *me*	ō	as in *no*	g	as in *go*

Abiathar	A-bī'-ä-thär	Jael	Jā'-el
Absalom	Ab'-sä-lom	Jericho	Je'-ri-kō
Achish	Ak'-ish	Jeroboam	Je-rō-bō'-am
Adoniram	A-dō-nī'-räm	Joab	Jō'-ab
Ahimelech	A-him'-ē-lek	Keilah	Kī'-lä
Akhenaten	A-ken-ä'-ten	Kirjath-Jearim	Kir'-yäth Je-är-im
Baal	Bä'-äl	Kishon	Ki'-shon
Beth-Shan	Beth-Shan'	Machir	Mä'-kēr
Beth-Shemesh	Beth-Shem'-esh	Megiddo	Mē-gid'-dō
Deborah	Deb'-ō-rä	Philistines	Fi-lis-tins
Delilah	Dē-li-lä	Rahab	Rā'-hab
El	El	Ramah	Rā'-mä
Eli	Ē'-lī	Rubudu	Roo-boo'-doo
Ebed-Hepa	E-bed-Hē'-pä	Seir	Sē'-er
Ephod	Ef'-od	Shiloh	Shī'-lō
Esdraelon	Ez'-drē-lon	Sisera	Sis'-e-rä
Gibeah	Gib'-ē-ä	Taanach	Tä'-ä-näk
Gibeon	Gib'-ē-on	Uriah	U-rī'-ä
Habiru	Hä-bē'-roo	Urusalim	Oo-roo'-sä-lim
Ish-Baal	Ish'-Bä-äl	Yahweh	Yä'-way
Issachar	Is'-sä-kär	Zebulon	Ze'-bū-lon
Jabesh-Gilead	Jā-besh-Gil'-e-ad	Ziklag	Zik'-lag

The Illustrations and Their Sources

THE WORLD THAT SURROUNDED THE HEBREWS. Prepared by Emily Denyse Wright and Harold W. Mallett. From *The Biblical Archaeologist*, February, 1940. Courtesy of Dr. G. Ernest Wright.

PHARAOH AKHENATEN. Courtesy of the Philadelphia Museum of Art.

A LETTER FROM EBED-HEPA. From *Tel-el-Amarna Tablets* (*Der Thontafelfund von El-Amarna*) by Winckler (Berlin: Hugo W. Spemann, 1889), figure 102.

AN ARAB CAMP. Underwood and Underwood.

JERICHO. From *The Story of Jericho*, by John Garstang (London, Hodder and Stoughton, 1934).

A CANAANITE FARMER. Carved sometime between 1350 and 1150 B.C.E. From *The Megiddo Ivories*, by Gordon Loud (Chicago: University of Chicago Press, 1939), plate 33. Courtesy of the Oriental Institute of the University of Chicago.

THE GOD BA-AL. The stone stele was found at Ras Shamra. The small figure in front of Ba-al is a worshiper. From an article by Johannes Friedrich, "Ras Shamra," in *Der Alte Orient*, Band 33, Heft ½, Tafel 2 (Leipzig: J. C. Hinrichs, 1933).

THE PLAIN OF ESDRAELON. View from the east. Courtesy of the Oriental Institute, Chicago.

CANAANITE CHARIOTEERS IN BATTLE. From *The Megiddo Ivories*. Courtesy of the Oriental Institute, Chicago.

CANAAN BEFORE THE HEBREW INVASION. Prepared by Calvin H. Schmitt. From *The Biblical Archaeologist*, September, 1940. Courtesy of Dr. G. Ernest Wright.

AN UNKNOWN HEBREW. From *Joshua* by Rogers MacVeagh and Thomas B. Costain (New York: Doubleday and Company, 1943). Courtesy of Doubleday and Company.

A LOOM LIKE DELILAH'S. It is probable that Delilah wove Samson's hair into the warp on such a loom and fastened it with the pin. When he awoke, "he plucked away the pin of the beam, and the web"

(Judges 16: 14). From *History of the Hebrew Commonwealth,* by Albert E. Bailey and Charles F. Kent (New York: Charles Scribner's Sons, 1924), page 83.

A PHILISTINE ALTAR OF INCENSE. From *Digging Up Biblical History,* by J. Garrow Duncan (New York: The Macmillan Company, 1931), Volume II, page 120. Courtesy of The Macmillan Company and the Society for Promoting Christian Knowledge.

PHILISTINES IN BATTLE. The swords are like those found in the ruins of Gaza. The shield designs are taken from Iron Age pottery, and the armor is copied from ancient Egyptian drawings of Philistine captive soldiers. From *The Foundations of Bible History: Joshua, Judges,* by John Garstang (London: Constable and Company, 1931), page 313.

AN ASIATIC NOMAD. From *Ancient Egyptian Paintings,* by Nina M. Davies (Chicago: University of Chicago Press, 1936), plate XI. Courtesy of the Oriental Institute, Chicago.

A CANAANITE ARK. Now in Palestine Museum, and dated about 1050-1000 B.C.E. It is made of clay and adorned with figures of cherubim. Courtesy of the Oriental Institute, Chicago.

THE GORGE OF MICHMASH. From *History of the Hebrew Commonwealth,* page 89. Courtesy of Dr. Albert E. Bailey.

A KING OF MEGIDDO AND HIS MUSICIAN. The king's chair is adorned with figures of cherubim—lions with human heads. Courtesy of the Oriental Institute, Chicago.

A PHILISTINE GIANT. Drawn by Gertrude Levy. From *The Foundations of Bible History: Joshua, Judges,* by John Garstang (London: Constable and Company, 1931) page 343.

EGYPTIAN MUSICIANS PLAYING LYRES. From *Music of the Bible,* by Enoch Hutchinson (Boston: Gould and Lincoln, 1864), figure 16.

A FEAST GIVEN BY A NOBLEMAN OF MEGIDDO. From *The Megiddo Ivories.* Courtesy of the Oriental Institute, Chicago.

EGYPTIAN PIPERS AND A HARPIST. From *Music of the Bible,* by Enoch Hutchinson (Boston: Gould and Lincoln, 1864), frontispiece.

THE GORGE OF ADULLAM. Underwood and Underwood.

THE TAKING OF A WALLED CITY IN CANAAN. The fortress of Askalon taken by Rameses II. From *The Foundations of Bible History: Joshua, Judges,* figure 10.

A SACRIFICIAL ALTAR AT MEGIDDO. Courtesy of the Oriental Institute, Chicago.

A Procession of Egyptian Women. From *The Music of the Bible,* by John Stainer, figure 94. Courtesy of Novello and Company and the H. W. Gray Company.

A Horned Altar. Now in the Palestine Museum. Courtesy of the Oriental Institute, Chicago.

A Canaanite Woman of Rank. From *The Megiddo Ivories.* Courtesy of the Oriental Institute, Chicago.

Cedars on One of the Mountains of Lebanon. From *History of the Hebrew Commonwealth,* page 129. Courtesy of Dr. Albert E. Bailey.

A Canaanite Nobleman on Parade. From *The Megiddo Ivories.* Courtesy of the Oriental Institute, Chicago.

Lumbermen of Lebanon. About 1513-1292 B.C.E. From *History of the Hebrew Commonwealth,* page 138. Courtesy of Charles Scribner's Sons.

King Solomon's Temple. The view is from the east. From *The History of Art in Sardinia and Judea,* translated by I. Gonino from the French of Georges Perrot and Charles Chipiez (New York: A. C. Armstrong and Son, 1890), Volume I.

A Merchant Fleet. From *A History of Egypt,* by James Henry Breasted (New York: Charles Scribner's Sons, 1905). Courtesy of Charles Scribner's Sons.

The Great Altar for Burnt Offerings in the Temple Court. Drawn by Mangeant. From *The History of Art in Sardinia and Judea,* Volume I.

A Selected Bibliography

Abingdon Bible Commentary, The, edited by F. C. Eiselen, Edwin Lewis, and David G. Downey. (New York and Cincinnati: Abingdon Press, 1929.) A new commentary on the Bible is greatly needed —one that will incorporate all the significant archaeological findings of the past twenty years. Fortunately one is being prepared.

Albright, William F. *Archaeology and the Religion of Israel.* Baltimore: Johns Hopkins Press, 1942.

————. *From the Stone Age to Christianity.* Baltimore: Johns Hopkins Press, 1940.

Bailey, Albert E., and Kent, Charles F. *History of the Hebrew Commonwealth.* Revised edition. New York: Charles Scribner's Sons, 1949.

Bewer, Julius A. *The Literature of the Old Testament.* Revised edition. New York: Columbia University Press, 1947.

Burrows, Millar. *What Mean These Stones?* New Haven, Conn.: American Schools of Oriental Research, 1941.

Edwards, Margaret D. *Child of the Sun: A Pharaoh of Egypt.* Boston: Beacon Press, 1939.

Finegan, Jack. *Light from the Ancient Past.* Princeton, N. J.: Princeton University Press, 1947.

Flight, John W. *Moses: Egyptian Prince, Nomad Sheikh, Lawgiver.* Boston: Beacon Press, 1942.

Garstang, John. *The Heritage of Solomon.* London: Williams and Norgate, 1934.

————. *The Story of Jericho.* London: Hodder and Stoughton, 1934.

Glueck, Nelson. *The Other Side of the Jordan.* New Haven, Conn.: American Schools of Oriental Research, 1940.

————. *The River Jordan.* Philadelphia: Westminster Press, 1946.

Gordon, Cyrus. *The Living Past.* New York: John Day, 1941.

James, Fleming. *Personalities of the Old Testament.* New York and London: Charles Scribner's Sons, 1939.

Kent, Charles F. *The Student's Historical Bible,* volumes II and III. New York: Charles Scribner's Sons 1912, 1913.

McCown, Chester C. *The Ladder of Progress in Palestine.* New York and London: Harper and Brothers, 1943.

Meek, Theophile J. *Hebrew Origins.* New York and London: Harper and Brothers, 1936.

Olmstead, A. T. *History of Palestine and Syria.* New York and London: Charles Scribner's Sons, 1931.

Pfeiffer, Robert H. *Introduction to the Old Testament.* New York and London: Harper and Brothers, 1941.

MAGAZINES

Biblical Archaeologist, The. Published by the American Schools of Oriental Research, New Haven, Conn.

Bulletin of the American Schools of Oriental Research. New Haven, Conn.